Successful Researc Supervision

'A fabulous resource for graduate advisors.'

Eric Mazur, Harvard University

Successful Research Supervision offers a research-based practical framework for academics to be able to examine and further develop their effectiveness as research supervisors.

Research supervisors working in all levels of higher education must ensure that their students gain efficiencies from working as part of an effective cohort and develop high levels of interdisciplinary understanding and critical thought. To impart these disciplines effectively is essential for any successful research supervisor. From helping researchers to begin, to managing a project through to successful completion, this book guides the reader through a series of exercises to identify their individual strengths and weaknesses and then provides theoretically sound advice in a practical and easy-to-use format.

Successful Research Supervision is full of examples of the best practice from outstanding scientists, social scientists and humanities supervisors from both the UK and the USA.

This book will encourage and help academics to:

- expand their own repertoire and array of actions and responses, thus giving them the flexibility to meet different situations with ease and confidence;
- identify the optimum combination of approaches to best fit individual students;
- understand the influence of their own value and experiences in the choice of their approach to research students;
- choose the most appropriate combination of approaches for a particular curriculum or project;
- employ a neutral language for developing and assisting others.

It also provides policy makers and curriculum designers with practical guidelines for evaluating their work.

Anne Lee is an independent academic and was Senior Academic Development Adviser at the University of Surrey.

Successful Research Supervision

Advising students doing research

Anne Lee

Routledge
Taylor & Francis Group

LONDON AND NEW YORK

First published 2012
by Routledge
2 Park Square, Milton Park, Abingdon, Oxon OX14 4RN

Simultaneously published in the USA and Canada
by Routledge
711 Third Avenue, New York, NY 10017

Routledge is an imprint of the Taylor & Francis Group, an informa business

British Library Cataloguing in Publication Data
A catalogue record for this book is available from the British Library

Library of Congress Cataloging in Publication Data
Lee, Anne, Dr.
Successful research supervision : advising students doing research /
Anne Lee. – 1st ed.
     p. cm.
  1. Graduate students--Supervision of. 2. Faculty advisors.
  3. Dissertations, Academic. I. Title.
LB2371.L44 2011
378.1'794--dc22   2011001659

ISBN: 978-0-415-66352-6 (hbk)
ISBN: 978-0-415-66353-3 (pbk)
ISBN: 978-0-203-81684-4 (ebk)

Typeset in Galliard by
HWA Text and Data Management, London

MIX
Paper from
responsible sources
FSC
www.fsc.org   FSC® C004839

Printed and bound in Great Britain by
TJ International Ltd, Padstow, Cornwall

This book is dedicated to Tony

Contents

Figures

Tables

Boxes

Foreword

This is a research-based book offering a practical framework to help those who supervise research students in higher education. There are quotations throughout from experienced advisers and supervisors describing how they made the process work for them.

How to use this book

There are several ways to use the information contained here, and how you approach these pages depends upon the amount of time you have and the reason you picked up the book in the first place.

1 If you are a new academic taking part of a teaching qualification in research supervision, then you will find reading the whole book provides a helpful resource.
2 If you are an academic pressed for time, but you want some quick ideas to help you structure your work with research students, then the tables in Chapter 8 will give you an easily accessible set of practical tools.
3 If you are facing a difficult situation with a particular student or group of students, then it will be worth looking through the list of tables to find a heading that links to that particular situation.
4 If you are an academic developer thinking about how to develop a programme for your university, then the whole book will be of interest, but look particularly at the section in Chapter 2 'Using the framework to support compare and contrast, and expanding awareness' and the section in Chapter 9 entitled 'Development opportunities for research supervisors'.
5 If you are a policy maker seeking to enhance the research capability of your institution, then you can use the framework to plan and evaluate a programme of organisational development.

The terms 'supervisor', 'advisor', 'academic', 'tutor' and 'lecturer' are used interchangeably throughout the book to describe the academic who is supervising students doing research. In the USA the supervisor is frequently called an 'advisor' and I use this spelling to denote the more formal role. 'Adviser' is used to refer to the more informal additional supervision often provided on a goodwill basis.

Legal requirements and codes of practice vary across countries, cultures and time. Supervisors reading this book are advised to take particular care and seek further advice to make sure that they observe local legislation when recruiting students or dealing with issues that might lead to legal action.

Acknowledgements

I am grateful to my colleagues at the University of Surrey for providing the initial interviews and for their support to complete this work, to those at Harvard University for their thoughtful interviews and to those at the Learning Institute at the University of Oxford who have helped to develop this work in several ways. Rowena Murray first suggested this book when we were driving through the Trossachs in Scotland, a grand place for such a vision. The grant from SEDA that enabled me to take this work to South Africa, was also vital in opening the door to comments from many cultural perspectives.

Gerlese Åkerlind gave seminal feedback on my analysis in the first stages of the research for this book and both Trevor Welland and Helen Sterne provided a detailed critique at the end. Any errors that remain are mine alone. James Wisdom provided constant encouragement. There are now hundreds of academics who have participated with me in workshops on supervising research, and they have all made a significant contribution to the evolution of the framework described here, particularly those at Sveriges Lantbruksuniversitet (SLU) in Sweden.

Finally I would like to thank Pam Denicolo and Lewis Elton, pioneers in their fields, both of whom set me on this path.

Any feedback for future editions would be welcome and the author can be contacted via the publisher or through www.drannelee.wordpress.com

Abbreviations

AFHEA	Associate Fellowship of the Higher Education Academy
ALTC	Australian Learning and Teaching Council
BBSRC	Biotechnology and Biological Sciences Research Council
CETL	centres for excellence in teaching and learning
CGS	Council for Graduate Studies (North America)
CID	Carnegie Initiative on the Doctorate (USA)
CIPD	Chartered Institute of Personnel Development (UK)
CPA	critical path analysis
CPD	continuing professional development
CV	curriculum vitae
DDoGS	Deans and Directors of Graduate Studies (Australia)
EBL	enquiry-based learning
EdD	Doctor of Education
EngD	Doctor of Engineering
EPSRC	Engineering and Physical Sciences Research Council
HEA	Higher Education Academy
HEI	higher education institution
HDR	higher degrees in research
MPhil	Master of Philosophy
PDP	personal development planning
PhD	Doctor of Philosophy
PsychD	Doctor of Psychology
QAA	Quality Assurance Agency (UK)
RDF	researcher development framework
SEDA	Staff and Educational Development Association (UK)
SOTL	scholarship of teaching and learning
TAPPS	Training and Accreditation Programme for Postgraduate Students
UKCGE	United Kingdom Council for Graduate Education

Chapter 1

A framework for analysing approaches to teaching and supervision

It is the thesis of this book that introducing the student to research requires a holistic teaching and learning approach from the academic. This chapter introduces a conceptual and research-driven approach to supervising research students doing research. It looks at how the different approaches (functional, enculturation, critical thinking, emancipation and relationship development) can all be utilised to develop independence, skills in research and academic writing.

An academic who supervises students doing research might want to use this book for several reasons: pragmatically it will enable them to expand their own repertoire and mix of actions and responses, and thus be more flexible to meet different situations. After reading it, they will understand more deeply how their preferred approach to working with research students is influenced by their own values and experiences and have a neutral language for discussions with fellow academics and co-supervisors about how roles and responsibilities will be shared. Mastering the different aspects of the framework proposed here will enable them to be able to choose the most appropriate combination of approaches for a particular context, problem or time.

Institutionally this framework can be used to evaluate the environment in which students are being asked to do research. It enables the exploration of answers to questions such as: is there a holistic approach to the student experience; what ethical research practices are we implicitly and explicitly encouraging and how are we developing, managing and valuing our supervisors and advisors – the people who have the most direct impact on our students?

Introducing students to research is an exciting part of academic work and many research supervisors have helped in the journey that this book describes. The original interviews to develop the framework were carried out with doctoral supervisors, but in my experience of working with masters and undergraduate students, the themes are applicable to all levels of higher education, and maybe beyond.

Aims of this book

1 To provide a research-based, scholarly approach to working with students doing research
2 To offer a tool for analysing the needs of different students
3 To propose strategies for identifying a wide range of solutions to typical problems that both students and their supervisors may encounter
4 To provide key terms for further study
5 To prompt readers to think of avenues for the further development of themselves and their institutions.

The debate about the research–teaching nexus

This is a book about *how* to link teaching and research. The battle about *whether* the two can co-exist has been fought by those trying to move us beyond the research–teaching divide, and that fight continues at a policy level both nationally and internationally through research councils and higher education funding bodies. The discussion about *what* it means to link research and teaching (or rather: in how many ways the combination of research and teaching can be entwined and supported) is explored here, and this book itself exemplifies one way of embedding and including research in the practice of supervision.

The research–teaching nexus is a challenge for most academics and there are several ways of conceptualising it. Working at the research–teaching nexus can include introducing individual or group research projects into the curriculum, embedding research evidence into teaching practice, researching our own practice as academics and research supervision (Healey & Jenkins 2009, Jenkins, Healey & Zetter 2007, Trowler & Wareham 2008, Tosey 2008).

Research at the doctoral level has been defined as seeking a scholarly approach towards creating original knowledge (Koch Christensen 2005, Trafford & Leshem 2008, Holbrook *et al.* 2007). At masters level it is more focused on developing research skills and at undergraduate level it is often about encouraging constructivism and enquiry-led learning. Levy (2009) has produced a matrix of inquiry-based learning which differentiates different types of research by looking at who frames the questions (student or staff) and whether the inquiry is into existing knowledge or creating new knowledge, the argument that work in all four quadrants requires the student to develop research skills. Angela Brew argues that this spirit of research and enquiry should run through the experience of all students in higher education when she calls for a 'new model of students as academics' (2006: 31).

Susan Breau, an academic lawyer, demonstrates this in practice when she challenges and inspires all her students early in their courses by telling them 'there is a fight in my discipline about how law is made, and your research can make a difference' (Breau 2009).

The process of forming scholars and scholarly work is central to research supervision; we are increasingly demanding researcher skills from our undergraduates as well as postgraduates. It is argued that in this world of super-complexity where frames of reference change rapidly, an interdisciplinary response is required to complex problems and the most portable knowledge we can enable our students to acquire is how to investigate, conceptualise and create new solutions (Barnett 2000, 2004). This approach to research-driven learning (sometimes called 'enquiry-based learning' in undergraduate and masters' programmes) is unlikely to completely replace any curricula. As Pang and Marton have pointed out, if we are to look for variations, we have to know what we are varying *from:*

> By consciously varying certain critical aspects of the phenomena in question, while keeping other aspects invariant, a space of variation is created that can bring the learner's focal awareness to bear upon the critical aspects which makes it possible for the learner to experience the object of learning.
>
> (Pang & Marton 2005: 164)

We have to enable students to engage with both primary and secondary (interpreted experiences of others) learning (Jarvis 2006: 85), so the argument of this book is not that *all* learning is research driven – but that as students move through the higher education system to doctoral research or what the Bologna process calls the 'third cycle', learning is increasingly research driven (Jenkins, Healey & Zetter 2007), and that we can usefully encourage a disposition towards research in all our students.

Thirty years ago Boyer argued that the time has come to move beyond the 'old teaching versus research debate' (Boyer 1990: xii) and this book aims to move towards Hattie and Marsh's demand that:

> Universities need to set as a mission goal the improving of the nexus between research and teaching. The aim is to increase the circumstances in which good teaching and research have occasion to meet, and to provide rewards not only for better teaching or for better research, but for demonstrations of the integration between teaching and research.
>
> (Hattie & Marsh 1996: 533)

Whilst scholarly formation is central, we can usefully debate what prior experience helps students to make an easy transition from undergraduate to doctoral research. Lovitts found that students did not need to be intellectually brilliant, they needed only sufficient intelligence and if that level of intelligence was assured, other traits became more important. In her research the successful doctoral students exhibited a tolerance of ambiguity, resilience and a practical intelligence which enabled them to solve problems more independently (Lovitts 2008); these are all traits which can be developed by introducing research into the undergraduate curriculum. In their desire to bring teaching and research closer together, Healey and Jenkins have collected many case studies of introducing research into the undergraduate and masters' curricula across many disciplines (2009) and their report provides useful resources and forms a significant part of the recommended reading for this chapter.

The framework introduced in this chapter (see Table 1.1) is intended to enable the academic to analyse their own preferences, strengths and weaknesses. It is only a guide and the categories in practice are not necessarily as discrete as the table makes them appear; it is holistic in that it brings together psychological, sociological, philosophical and organisational theories and offers choices to academics. This conceptual approach can be adapted to deconstruct ways of dealing with a range of different problems and there are examples of applying the framework in an integrated way in Chapter 8, where the fluidity that is required to make the framework operate fully is explored. With the help of the framework described in this book, academics can analyse and plan which combination of approaches is likely to help which students, they no longer have to rely only upon anecdotes, trial and error or their own experience as students, neither do they need only to reflect upon their experience with their colleagues (perhaps as a second supervisor) to be able to choose what to do when meeting their students doing research.

This work is aimed at the academic who is supervising students doing research at any level. The research for this book was originally carried out with postgraduate supervisors but the principles can also be applied wherever research is introduced into the curriculum. Thus this book addresses the research–teaching nexus in a new way, it argues that the skills that are required to nurture and supervise doctoral students, have the same core as those required to supervise larger groups of students at different levels.

The scholarship of teaching and learning (SOTL) refers both to an ancient art of education and the emerging fields still occupying contested ground. The journey so far has taken us from Boyer's principles of discovery, integration, application and teaching (1990) to the values of the UK professional body 'Staff and Educational Development Association' (SEDA). These values include a commitment to understanding how people learn; a questioning and analytical approach using appropriate theoretical tools to continually improve practice within an ethically based context; a commitment to work in and develop learning communities, promoting inclusivity and personal reflection (SEDA 2003). More recently there has been a growing understanding that disciplinary pedagogical practices differ (Golde & Walker 2006, Golde 2007, Entwistle 2007) and need to be catered for and in the UK this has been exemplified by the Higher Education Academy establishing some vibrant subject centre networks.

Table 1.1 A framework of approaches to research supervision (adapted from Lee 2008 a and b)

Professional → Personal

	Functional	Enculturation	Critical thinking	Emancipation	Relationship development
Supervisor's activity	• Rational progression through tasks • Consultation • Techno-rational	• Gatekeeping • Introductions to people and exemplars of high quality work	• Evaluation • Challenge • Enquiry-based partnership	• Mentoring • Supporting constructivism	• Supervising by experience • Developing a relationship/team
Supervisor's knowledge and skills	• Directing • Leading • Negotiating • Project management	• Diagnosis of deficiencies • Coaching	• Argument • Analysis • Synthesis	• Facilitation • Reflection	• Managing conflict • Emotional intelligence
Possible student reaction	• Logical • Information giving • Organised • Obedient	• Role modelling • Apprenticeship	• Constant inquiry • Synthesis • Fight or flight	• Personal growth • Reframing	• A good team member • Emotional intelligence

A brief history of learning through research

Architects of education from Socrates to Dewey have battered the door of didactic pedagogy. The introduction of problem-based learning and initiatives to include research in the undergraduate curriculum conveys a contemporary ideal to engage students in discovery learning. As we have seen, the supervision of students doing research is most familiar to academics at the doctoral level and it was Wilhelm Von Humboldt, the eminent philosopher of liberalism and Prussian Minister for Education who proposed a new type of doctorate to be awarded for original research. The first modern doctorate was awarded in 1810 (Taylor 2009) and it was soon exported. Oxford offered the first PhD in the UK in 1917 and in spite of concerns about the abilities of the students, many other UK universities soon set up Research Committees and offered this degree (Simpson 2009).

More recently universities have been establishing Graduate Schools where masters and doctoral students will be expected to complete and defend their dissertations and theses. These Graduate Schools (sometimes also known as Doctoral Training Centres) have many guises (Denicolo *et al.* 2010), but a key feature of them all is that they convey a sense of embracing the academic elite. They have been supported by national bodies such as the UK Council for Graduate Education (UKCGE) which was established in 1994 and which claims to be 'an authoritative voice for the HE sector on postgraduate activity in the UK' (www.ukcge.ac.uk) or the North American 'Council for Graduate Schools', established over 40 years ago, which says it is 'the only national organization in the United States that is dedicated solely to the advancement of graduate education and research' (see http://www.cgsnet.org). A new study started in 2010 is currently being carried out on the challenges facing doctoral education funded by a grant from the Australian Learning and Teaching Council (ALTC) and working in partnership with the Australian Deans and Directors of Graduate Studies (DDoGS). It aims to look at where research students are coming from and why. (See further details at http://www.altc.edu.au/november2010-new-partnership-focusing-higher-degree-reseach)

In any case we have moved far beyond supervision as it was in the last century. The historian, Renate Simpson, reminded us of how Ernest Rutherford (the father of nuclear physics) made it a habit to tour the whole laboratory once a day and have a word with each student. Whereas when Henry A. Rowland (the first president of the American Physical Society) at Johns Hopkins was asked what he was planning to do with his students that day: 'Do with them? Do with them?' he retorted, 'I shall neglect them' (Simpson 2009: 29).

Some trends in research education at PhD level

The Bologna Process aims for the harmonisation of educational qualifications across Europe, and this ambitious programme has had ramifications internationally as more countries want to participate in working towards having qualifications that are seen as having comparable status internationally. Economic pressures have contributed towards an increasing focus on the need for research degrees to be completed within a defined time-frame, while the student body has become more internationally mobile, diverse and part-time. The skills agenda has surfaced (see Chapter 8), fuelled by concerns about the employability of research students, and the numbers of professional doctorates offered (e.g. Eng D, Psych D, Ed D) has increased amidst some concern about the comparable quality of research degrees. English has become the language for higher research degrees and there are calls for monitoring research from the perspective of international security issues.

Stan Taylor has coined these developments as 'ations' and points to massification, globalisation, diversification, commodification, McDonaldisation, regulation, capitalisation and multiplication as all having implications for the supervisory process. He argues that there is an increased obligation for the supervisor to support international and diverse groups of students, and that consumerisation has raised student expectations to complete on time and acquire generic skills whilst supervisors need to be fully aware of university and legal obligations and regulations (Taylor 2009).

How can we problematise pedagogical practices in research supervision?

The discourse of pedagogy invites us to consider the many layers and aspects involved in teaching and learning, and whilst this book problematises and focuses on the relationship between academic(s) and student(s), there is an important wider context which is referred to below. Definitions can be restrictive as well as illuminative and the broader definition of pedagogy as 'any conscious activity by one person designed to enhance learning in another' (Mortimore 1999: 3) opens the door to our examination of this term. There are *pedagogical practices* in research supervision (e.g. developing academic literacy; using posters to summarise different stages of the research process; adapting and developing signature pedagogies for different disciplines and planning to work within a diverse, multi-cultural and international framework – Walker & Thomson 2010). Pedagogical activities vary according to context – the academic discipline and the nature of the university are two key parts of this context, other elements are influenced by the social structure, resources, time, pacing and goals (Mortimore 1999). These and many other aspects are explored further later in this book and can be found in the examples that are given of different approaches to dealing with a variety of issues that can arise.

Liberating or controlling?

Education can be a liberating, humanistic, self-actualising endeavour, or it can be a performative, skills-based and employability-driven task. In some cases one can lead to the other. It can move from the performative to the liberal because mastering a skill or profession can give the self-confidence and experience to seek to learn more. It can move from the liberal to the performative because uncovering an inner motivation can give the energy to learn how to master a skill or profession. The works of Dewey, Bruner and Ciari (Leach & Moon 2008) all indicate the power of problem-based education rooted in the exploration of issues that students are currently experiencing and that they find compelling. Freire (1970), in his powerful book *The Pedagogy of the Oppressed*, described the phenomena of 'banking' where the student is seen as an empty vessel to be filled with knowledge that is relatively static. He contrasted 'banking' (which he saw as a negative pedagogic attitude) with problem-posing education where dialogue between the educator and the student is essential and the relationship becomes more about the shared investigation. The framework proposed in this book implies that the academic can in practice successfully embrace multiple perspectives on power and education, whilst perhaps holding one ultimate value most dear (and for many academics that is probably a value akin to student empowerment).

Another aspect of pedagogy which can be both liberating and controlling is what I have called 'the maturational approach'. An example of this is the observations of Piaget, where he noted the different stages of child development; Perry (1970), Baxter Magolda (1992) and Belenky *et al.* (1986) have done similar work in charting adults' stages of knowing. The underlying theme of this approach is authoritative ('I know where you are going'), but it can also be empowering. Pedagogical concepts such as 'scaffolding and fading', 'threshold concepts', 'deep and surface learning', 'learning taxonomies' all fall into this category (see Biggs & Tang 2007, Murray 2008, Mortimore 1999 and Daniels 2008 for further explanations of some of these issues).

A social or a cognitive process?

Many readers will instantly see this question as a false dichotomy. However, it enables us to ask whether we are giving due attention to both the social construction of knowledge, the society and the culture(s) that the student is working within, as well as pushing at the door that is being increasingly opened by neuroscientists looking at learning and the skills of critical analysis that we seek to develop in students doing research. A good example of this work is by Turner and Curran (2006) who used neuroscience to explain why the social and emotional aspects of learning ('the successful engagement of emotional attention', p. 5) are so important when they linked student's comments on how they learned to the release of dopamine in the brain. They also comment on the negative effect that excess stress can have on learning by linking it to the amygdala which drives cognitive programmes from the complex to the simple.

Critical thinkers concentrate on the development of the brain and its ability to examine knowledge philosophically. Those who see research pedagogy as a social process will be keen to examine the assumptions that might be made by different groups of people, and they may also be keen to harness the power of groups in learning activities. They will be interested in the power bases that are supported by various groups and the ways that these power bases mould how we see what we see. Those who see research pedagogy primarily as a cognitive process may come from a more scientific and experimental paradigm and would include those who have studied behaviourism, stimulus–response behaviour modification and who focus on extrinsic motivation. This book argues that effective research supervision (no matter what the discipline) needs to take both approaches into account.

An organisational or an individual activity?

There are a few examples of researchers who are working and learning entirely on their own. However, the fact that there are few of them (and even those who are working independently are frequently retired from earlier academic careers) exposes the norm – which is that most of the students who do research are working within an academic or other type of organisation. As soon as that organisational umbrella is embraced, it brings with it opportunities, procedures, quality assurance processes and local, national and sometimes global politics.

There has been a focus on the need to master tacit knowledge if one is to survive and thrive in organisations (Eraut 2007) but other related concepts include organisational strategy, behaviour and change, organisational development (e.g. appreciative inquiry), markets, customers, managerial and entrepreneurial environments.

Learning in different universities, in spite of the efforts of the Bologna process to harmonise education across Europe, continues to be a variable experience. The academic–student ratio is fundamental to the learning experience, yet league tables show us how widely it can vary (in the Independent's 2010/2011 edition it ranged from 9 students to one member of staff at University College London to 37:1 at the University for the Creative Arts (see www.thecompleteuniversityguide.co.uk). Gibbs (2010) warns us that low staff/student ratios do not guarantee close contact (it is difficult from the sorts of figures given above to identify academic from administrative staff, or to know how much time is spent on teaching and how much on research) but they do make it possible. Economists have measured a negative effect on the exam results of postgraduate students studying at MSc in larger classes. More specifically, they note that students moving from small (1–19) to medium-sized groups (20–33) and those studying in classes of over 100 will get significantly poorer exam results. This is particularly significant given that the numbers of postgraduate students is increasing at a greater rate than both the numbers of undergraduate students and the numbers of academics to teach them (Bandiera, Larcinese & Rasul 2010). Arguably the Oxbridge tutorial system, which some see as a 'pedagogic gem' (Palfreyman 2008), provides students with individual or small group research supervision from their first term as an undergraduate, yet other universities can find it almost impossible to offer their undergraduates any individual supervision or tutoring at all. We also know that within the same university the research priorities and environment can change and that can have a dramatic impact on the resources available to support students doing research (Drake & Heath 2011: 15).

The humanist (and individual) approach to pedagogy argues that process is important and that learners must define their own agenda. This is obviously a part of the researching student's experience and explains why such research can be a powerful experience; however, it can lead to such specialism that there is patchy curriculum coverage.

Supervision one-to-one or as part of an academic team?

Whilst much of this book focuses on the single academic and their relationship with their research student(s), there is a growing awareness that there is usually a team of academics and administrative assistants involved in research supervision (Lee 2008b, Manathunga & Goozee 2007, Watts 2010). There are also wider influences outside the department that can have an impact on the student's ability to complete their research (McAlpine & Norton 2006).

The way that the departmental academic and administrative team work together (or not) can affect the student's experience both positively and negatively. Whether the team members see themselves as in a hierarchy (maybe one mentoring another), a collegial team of equals or (sadly) in competition with each other, will also affect the supervision experience for the academic. Most universities now require at least one supervisor in the team to have seen a doctoral student through to completion. Where roles are clear and relationships are good, teams can create a positive and enjoyable situation. Ideally shared supervision can result in an appropriate division of skills and knowledge, and a helpful learning experience for the academics as well as the students. There are many advantages to team-working when it is going well: the principle supervisor can delegate some functions, newer supervisors can learn new skills, personality clashes can be more diffused, if one supervisor leaves the student will not be so bereft, and problems can be shared and sometimes more creatively solved.

However, where team supervision is not working so well, there can be additional problems: if roles are not allocated clearly then all the academics can think that the student and their research is mostly 'someone else's responsibility', students can be confused by receiving apparently conflicting advice and apparently different approaches to supervision. It is certainly true that team meetings can take time.

Just as research supervision can be viewed as providing a close-up look at aspects of pedagogy, so team supervision can be viewed as providing a close-up look at how departmental academic teams can work together on a range of academic endeavours. The role of administrative staff in supporting students can also have a profound effect on their work, and they too should be included in team meetings. Introducing a team to the framework proposed in this book can provide a neutral language for discussing roles and responsibilities within the academic team.

The tools of research and their influence on pedagogy

Activity theorists suggest that we should look for internal contradictions and tension points and instinctively know that the tools employed in any activity also shape and form it. The tools involved in research pedagogy include laboratories (where team-work and collegiality become more evident), simulations and employment-based opportunities for research (where students studying for professional doctorates or masters in business administration will frequently spend a great deal of time); the availability and accessibility of on-line resources, teaching spaces such as lecture theatres and seminar rooms, and web-based learning opportunities all help to fashion the available pedagogical approach (Engstrom 1996, 2001, Savin-Baden 2008). On-line journal clubs are being experimented with and web 2 technology facilitates international collaboration. The availability of these tools and the attitude towards using them will affect the student's attitude towards and ability to do research.

A scholarly approach requires a critical stance. The problematising of issues around teaching and supervision at a high level has frequently looked at the power relationships using metaphors to describe this process. The metaphor of the master–slave relationship has been described by Grant (2005), and Lee and Green (2009) summarise research which talks about the 'arche-metaphors' of apprenticeship, discipleship and authorship. They argue that these are limiting, westernised concepts. Whilst these analyses of power are an undercurrent in the framework described here, the research for this book has uncovered other elements at play and aims to broaden, interrogate and transform these metaphors into more tangible approaches to supervising students who research. The traditional power model has been made more complex by the introduction of student fees and pressures on doctoral students to complete. Students are more litigious and can threaten to sue universities for providing inadequate teaching or research supervision. The relationship between student and academic is much debated, but the notions of student as consumer or supplicant are unhelpful because they make education a commodity. The student as co-inquirer or co-producer of knowledge is often more acceptable (Watson 2009) and leads to a relationship of critical partnership where both need to be able to articulate expectations of each other and negotiate compromises. Thus one test of the holistic nature of the framework in this book could be: if the academic was reasonably competent in each approach in this framework, and flexible in its application, would this create a good enough experience for the student?

Another way of testing the framework is to imagine yourself as the student and ask: 'if my professor could articulate what she or he could and could not do for me in the terms of the framework – would that define an acceptable learning contract?'

Introducing the framework

This framework arose out of researching the conceptual models that academics have when supervising research students (Lee 2008a, 2008b), and just as research has found variations in students' approaches to learning, it has also found variations in academics' perceptions of context when teaching. There are also links *between* students' approaches to learning and teachers' approaches to teaching (Ramsden 2003, Prosser & Trigwell 1999). Cause and effect have still to be explored, but we can surmise that the academics' approach to creating a research environment will have an impact on how a student will do their research, and that the academics' approach to teaching will have an impact on how those students develop.

This framework enables examination of different values, beliefs and concepts. Its underlying premise is that an experienced academic will be able to move through and to any area, and, in relation to thesis writing, will set tasks as they become appropriate. As the student gains competence from each perspective they will move through learning about the knowledge and philosophy behind their discipline to becoming an instinctive thinker in the manner of their discipline, or to put it another way, they will start by understanding the epistemology of their discipline and move to embody an ontological perspective.

Five main approaches were identified. They intertwine in a complex manner and, although they are disentangled here to aid clarity, it is not maintained that they are independent of each other.

The new academic will want to concentrate on mastering the processes involved in the functional approach, but once they are mastered they (and their students) will gain immeasurably from working with the other approaches as well.

I have already argued that the framework is holistic and integrative, it includes organisational, sociological, philosophical, psychological and emotional dimensions, I also suggest that there is an overarching tension between the professional and the personal which surfaces particularly in the academic's role as a supervisor or advisor. If the academic is using a functional approach, they will be acting professionally, if they are working from a place of a mutual relationship, then they will be acting more from their personal self. Both selves can combine and provide perfectly satisfactory supervision, but from the research it appears that the academic who is outstanding will be able to work from any of the five approaches as it becomes appropriate.

Table 1.1 introduces the framework and provides the foundation for the analysis that follows throughout the book. The framework illustrates the different conceptual approaches that lie behind the ways that supervisors might approach their research students. The functional approach will require a timetable, clear objectives and regular meetings. The enculturation approach will focus on encouraging the research student to become a member of a research community, to understand and apply the methods of good practice in the discipline. The critical thinking approach will concentrate on the research inquiry and how it contributes original knowledge. The emancipatory approach concentrates on the personal growth and journey of the research student and the relationship approach focuses on creating an emotionally intelligent relationship between supervisor(s) and student(s).

These different approaches are complementary, and the boundaries between them are permeable. They form a useful basis for disaggregating different beliefs and actions in the teaching and the supervisory processes.

A 'research cycle' has been formulated which aims to identify the common core phases, activities and tasks (functions) across disciplines. These are: framing (and reframing) the research proposal; negotiating entry to be able to access data; generating the data and ideas; creating results, models, designs and artifacts; disseminating and reflecting (Macfarlane 2009). In Table 1.2 we can see the framework used to explore a range of approaches to carrying out these tasks.

One criticism of the framework proposed in this book is that it aims to create too much of a 'tidy reconciliation' of a process which is undeniably messy and individual. However, the original objective of the research project was to identify the concepts which would make learning about supervision easier. The 'messiness' is still apparent when it comes to combining, blending and applying the different approaches to individual situations, which is explored further in Chapter 8.

Encouraging creativity

In Chapter 8, I also look at how the framework can enable academics to create and then choose from a range of actions and reactions when supervising

Table 1.2 Using the framework to explore approaches to the different phases of the research cycle

Functional phases of managing research	Enculturation	Critical thinking	Emancipation	Relationship development
Framing	Looking at other examples in the discipline	Asking: what is excluded? what is assumed? Completing a risk analysis	Assessing where this approach could take the student, both professionally in their career and personally	Discussing whether this is something that 'we can work on together'
Negotiating	Asking who else in the department or discipline is doing similar work? What opportunities for collaboration might there be? What contacts might be approached?	Looking at collaboration and links to work in or across other disciplines	Who else in society might be usefully included or involved in this work?	Discussions about the tenor of the approaches to be made and how to negotiate effectively
Generating	By reviewing the research methods most commonly used in the discipline Looking for opportunities for joint fieldwork	By identifying and arguing for the most appropriate research methods. Creating new research methods	By exploring and understanding the methodological imperatives behind different approaches to research and the implications of these approaches	By sharing own research methods, experiences and concerns
Creating	Through team discussion By analysing data, looking for advances in the field	By creating new models and theories and critiquing their generalisability	By linking advances to areas of personal growth	By sharing the interpretative process
Disseminating	Through departmental seminars and conferences	Through conference discussions, responding to referees' reports, writing journal publications and books Further grant applications	Through performance and open discussions Wider publications (not necessarily just academic journals)	Shared publications and presentations
Reflecting	On epistemological progress On how the team supported and were involved in the research process	On how knowledge is created/discovered On the appropriateness or otherwise of the implicit and explicit frameworks employed	On impact on self and ontological development	On impact on relationship development and ability to work productively. Also assessing the impact on friends and family

students who research. At this stage I want to look at how the framework can be used to explore one of the core elements of research: creativity. At levels 6–8 (UK National Framework) or the Bologna description of the 'second and third cycles' (bachelors to PhD level) it is apparent that there is international agreement that being creative is a key activity for all research students: at the bachelors level this falls within the requirement to be able to solve problems in complex and unpredictable circumstances, at the masters level students are required to demonstrate originality in their application of knowledge and at the doctoral level there is a requirement to create original knowledge (QAA 2008, Dublin Descriptors JQI 2004).

Creativity is also a personal construct and is one of the areas where understanding needs to be created between supervisor and student. How quickly should a student doing research be introduced to this supervisor's construct? (For an explanation of supervisors' quotes to disciplinary groups see Table 2.1)

> For me, creativity is when we walk between two worlds, the metaphysical and the physical. (Soft pure)

Kleiman has drawn a phenomenological map of creativity in learning and teaching (2008: 211) and Hargreaves (coming from a nursing background) argues that we need to encourage creativity, but identifies a tension between creativity and managing risk (Hargreaves 2008).

Sternberg and Lubart (1995) argue that creativity requires various intelligences (synthetic, analytic and practical) and a mixture of psychological, intellectual and environmental opportunities. They write about how important a level of knowledge is if we are to be able to discern what is truly creative and original, and they explore other issues such as motivation, thinking skills, persistence, and an optimum environment.

Originality is going to be judged first by those within the discipline, so there is an enculturation element in the types of challenges we set:

> I gave her a problem I honestly thought would form a very large part of her PhD it was so challenging. And she came back literally the next day and said she'd thought of a solution and would I like to see it. And she had done it! (Hard applied)

In this case the supervisor went on to explain what the challenge was in supervising such an able student:

> I think it was close to brilliant I would say. It was incredibly inspired. And she went on to do some very significant things. I would say she was so bright than even in papers she was publishing some of the reviewers struggled to understand the subtleties of what she was saying. In her

particular case my main focus was how to develop her communication skills and how to present material, because there was no question she was right, it was just a question that other people often had difficulty understanding where she was coming from with it.

Enabling creativity and originality is a crucial test of research supervision. It is quite possible for the research student to be encouraged to be creative in any of the approaches to study (see Table 1.3). This could be seen as moving along the suggested dimensions of creativity as a constraint-focused experience to a fulfilment-processed experience (Kleiman 2008: 212). It is also useful to consider how creativity is engendered in supervision alongside academics' perceptions of how knowledge is created in their subject (see Chapter 5). Table 1.3 represents only the beginning of an important debate which is continued in different ways through the various chapters of this book.

One analysis of how each approach might encourage creativity is shown below, and perhaps one of the more surprising elements to emerge is that the functional approach can also encourage creativity. An example of this arose in an interview with a supervisor from outside the scientific paradigm (which is significant because in laboratories it is common for teams to work long hours) who said:

I think they find the direction difficult, that I have been so directive. I think they thought that they could swan in and wander around the literature for a bit and do what they liked ... so I have insisted that they are here 9am – 5pm five days a week. That is very hard for them ... I am beginning to think the structure helps to make creativity, I would never have believed I would have said that. I think it is because people know where the boundaries are, they know what they have got to achieve and this helps in achieving that ... they are putting up (creative ideas) on the wall ... there is a sense of freedom in the structure I think. (Soft applied)

Table 1.3 Approaches to supervision and encouraging creativity

Creativity as constraint focused .... Creativity as fulfilment focused				
Functional	**Enculturation**	**Critical thinking**	**Emancipation**	**Relationship development**
Creativity might arise from:				
A reaction or resistance to constraints	A process of incremental change	Purpose exploitation of chance occurrences	Reaction to disorientation	Creating something new that has personal value

Structure was far from this next academic's mind when answering the question about how to enable creativity; these two quotations demonstrate a blending of critical thinking and emancipation in developing creativity:

> Critical reflexivity is vital to enable breaking down rigid constructs. A PhD student's problem is that they read what they already know, and read about opposing positions to discredit it. So they will shuffle the cards, and talk about different methodologies and get the same or different results. But that is level 7 thinking because it does not dissolve these constructs. (Soft pure)

('Level 7 thinking' refers to masters' level programmes in the QAA's Framework for Higher Education Qualifications: QAA 2008).

Critical thinking is also apparent here:

> I have one mature student who is a senior partner in (his organisation), and it is great being his supervisor, he is so on the ball. Part of me thinks 'what on earth have I got to offer him'? Then it turns out that he is breaking new ground himself and he really wants somebody else who thinks in very bizarre ways, which is what I do. (Soft pure)

Many are used to juxtaposing the concepts of emancipation and creativity, but the reaction to constraints and criticism can also force the formation of new ideas. Table 1.3 uses Kleiman's work to illustrate how different approaches to supervision might encourage creativity.

In this chapter I have introduced the rationale behind this book: that it aims to exemplify one way of holding the tension between research and teaching by creating an evidence-based framework for supervising students who research.

I have also introduced the framework itself and demonstrated how it can be used to look at supervisor approaches, possible student reactions and to engender creativity. The recommended reading for this chapter includes a theoretical study of the research–teaching nexus by Angela Brew, a practical report full of examples of how research can be introduced into the undergraduate curriculum by Alan Jenkins and Mick Healey and a book by Daniel Pratt, whose framework of teaching also suggested five different approaches which could be related to this work and help those who want to explore links between research supervision and teaching styles.

The next chapter looks at alternative models of supervision and the research behind the framework that has just been introduced.

The subsequent five chapters look in more detail at each of the five approaches, both from the interview data and from the literature that the interview data indicated as relevant, and these are followed by a summary of how the framework can be used to analyse some common problems from different points of view in Chapter 8.

The Salzburg Principles arose from a European seminar on doctoral programmes and they include encouraging professional development and employability as key themes for doctoral research (Koch Christensen 2005). In the UK, ring-fenced money has been allocated to universities to support skills development for postgraduate researchers (Roberts 2002). In the final chapter I address how these initiatives could be developed to support the emergence of the globally competent postgraduate. That chapter addresses possible goals for extending and developing skills training for postgraduates and supervisor development. At the end of Chapter 9 is a glossary of key terms organised according to the framework which, in addition to the further reading suggested at the end of various chapters, will help those who are interested in further study of the different approaches.

Further reading

Brew, A. (2006) *Research and Teaching, Beyond the Divide*. Basingstoke: Palgrave Macmillan.

Healey, M. and Jenkins, A. (2009) *Developing Undergraduate Research and Inquiry*. York: Higher Education Academy.

Pratt, D. T. (1998) *Five Perspectives on Teaching in Adult and Higher Education*. Malabar, FL: Krieger.

Chapter 2

The emergence of
the framework

Alternative models of research supervision

There are now a range of models for looking at research supervision. Gatfield (2005) based his research on the Blake and Mouton Managerial Grid model, and verified his work through 12 in-depth interviews with supervisors. He found two axes of 'support' and 'structure' and argued that where support and structure are low the academics' style was found to be laissez-faire, and where support and structure were high, there was a contractual style. A pastoral style would mean that the academic provided high personal support but left the student to manage the structure of their research project and the directorial style would do the reverse. Gatfield argues (as I do) that no one approach is right or wrong, it is about appropriateness and sharing expectations.

In Figure 2.1, I show an outline of Gatfield's model with some of the elements of the framework described in this book superimposed in italics on

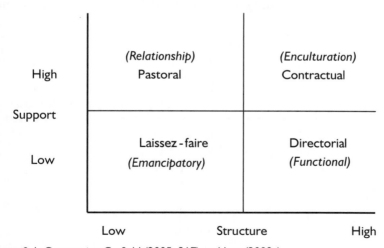

Figure 2.1 Contrasting Gatfield (2005: 317) and Lee (2008a)

it. From this much simplified summary of Gatfield's work we can see that it does not explicitly address the issue of critical thinking. It is also doubtful whether we can superimpose the other terms directly on the framework, for example the terms such as 'low structure' and 'emancipatory' are not really the same.

Murphy *et al.* (2007) produced another four-quadrant matrix from interviews with 17 engineering supervisors and their students (34 participants in total) which looked at guiding and controlling on one axis and person and task focus on the other. Murphy and her colleagues also make the observation that supervision models are linked to beliefs about teaching, and this view is backed up by the research for this book.

Murphy usefully creates detailed descriptions of each of the quadrants that her model creates and she analyses them along many factors including role of supervisor, role of candidate, outcomes, decision-making and focus. Again, if we plot the framework in this book against the axis proposed by Murphy *et al.* (see Figure 2.2) we see some of the differences; in Murphy's model there is potentially a conflation of two elements: functional and critical thinking.

In this instance the conflation is between a core task of supervision (developing critical thinking) and the functional task of the institution (achieving completion on time within quality assurance measures). Similar reservations to those expressed in the comparison with the Gatfield model remain about aligning the terms 'low control' and 'emancipatory' and 'high control' and 'enculturation'.

These two models provide a useful contrast to the framework proposed in this book, but a four-quadrant matrix is more limiting in terms of analysis. The framework proposed here is multi-dimensional: it has five approaches analysed in a large number of ways (e.g. values, independency to dependency, developing creativity, lecturing and curriculum design). The proposal that

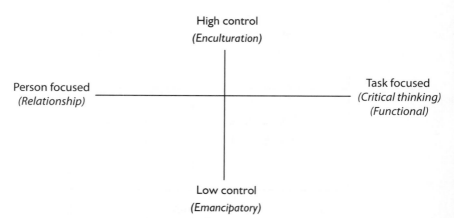

Figure 2.2 An interpretation of Murphy et al.'s model (2007) contrasted with Lee (2008a)

I am making here is that as many elements as possible should become transparent to both the academic and the postgraduate student.

A second, frequently described approach was created originally by Acker who looked at the 'technical rational model' (where the goal is either the creation of an independent researcher, scholarly creativity or speedy completion) and contrasted it with the 'negotiated order model' where there are 'many unspoken agendas operating throughout the research process and mutual expectations are subject to negotiation and change over time' (Acker quoted in Wisker 2005: 27). This approach problematises supervision and links to the functional approach described later in this book.

Grant and others have used a small number of cases of masters and doctoral supervision, analysed the dialogue and described power dynamics of the Hegelian 'master–slave' or 'apprenticeship' models (Grant 2005, 2008). A development of this approach moves the focus away from the supervisor/ student dyad and looks at the practices implied by the model of 'communities of practice' (Lave & Wenger 1991) – this is, in effect, offering a decentralised version of the master/apprentice role. Lave and Wenger's work has had great impact in highlighting sociological issues implicit in teaching and learning, and they explore the way in which the student is helped (or not) to move through legitimate peripheral participation to an understanding and mastery of the tacit knowledge required to participate fully in an academic community. This element is explored further in the 'enculturation' approach to teaching and supervision (see Chapter 4).

Lovitts argues that the components needed for creative work are: domain-relevant skills (intelligence and knowledge), creativity (thinking styles and personality) and task motivation. She also identifies the micro and macro environments that the student is operating in, and argues that the micro environment (in particular the relationship between student and their advisor) is the most important (Lovitts 2008).

It has been argued that engaging in supervision and teaching requires a process of self-transformation, and this reinforced the idea that successful supervision is a function of a fully integrated self (Firth & Martens 2008). This is a feminist and post-colonial critique which argues that identity fragmentation is dehumanising. Whilst a noble aim, it is also a utopian ideal for some. The purpose of this book is to help the reader to become a 'good enough' supervisor or teacher and not to require the academic to have to engage in personal odysseys in order to become competent.

Halse and Malfroy (2010) have retheorised doctoral supervision as professional work and linked it conceptually with Aristotle's intellectual virtues. They include *phronesis* (habits of the mind), which is a combination of critical thinking and engagement; *episteme* (theoretical knowledge acquired through reflection and thinking) by which they mean fruitful participation in scholarly expertise by producing articles and scholarly papers and *techne* which relates to the capacity to write and communicate, use scientific resources, manage information and time. They also refer to the obligations of the learning alliance (the agreement between the student and supervisor) which has resonance with work on the therapeutic alliance and is discussed further in Chapter 7.

Cumming (2010) has produced an integrative model of doctoral enterprise which locates doctoral practices in their wider context – both within the institution and within society more widely. He has produced a useful matrix (2010: 33) that enables analysis of doctoral work in four areas: the curriculum, the pedagogical tools, the research itself and the work of publishing, teaching, producing and contributing. This matrix still creates a list of tasks that the supervisor needs to master, but it also illuminates it by looking at practical understandings, rules and principles, teleoaffective structures and general understandings. His argument (like mine) is that his model enables a more holistic approach and mitigates against the more instrumental approach towards doctoral education that seems to be emerging across the sector.

The research for this book

Methods and samples

A variety of methods have been used to explore both the generalisability of the proposed framework and the acceptability and range and depth of information that each method produced. Some of the methods came from traditional qualitative research methods. The original interviews with academics took place in a research-led university in the UK, and subsequent interviews took place with academics at Harvard University, USA and at other research-led universities in the UK. In addition an experiential element has been added: many workshops have taken place in Sweden, Estonia, Denmark and the UK between 2007 and 2011. Interviews and focus groups with students took place over the same period. The poster session also took place during a teaching and learning conference in 2008. The study was given approval by the UK university's ethics committee and was conducted in accordance with the British Psychological Society's Code of Practice.

One significant difference between this book and the work of many other authors is that there was a balance of interviewees between scientific and social science disciplines. Others have concentrated more on arts and social science disciplines (for example: Grant 2005, Wisker 2005, Hockey 1994, 1996).

Stage 1: qualitative interviews

The framework was first created from an analysis of interviews with 12 UK academics and focus groups with 20 students (not necessarily from the same pairs). The sample of academics was purposive: excellent supervisors from across a range of disciplines were interviewed. There were four female and eight male academics. The sample of students was opportunistic, but included masters and doctoral students from soft and hard applied subjects and soft pure subject groups.

The framework was extended and deepened with further interviews: three supervisors at Harvard (they call them 'advisors') were all male and they came from pure hard and applied disciplines. Subsequent interviews have taken place in the UK with more female academics and those working in the humanities and arts to balance the sample. In the next chapter Table 3.1 shows a sample of 20 interviewees, their disciplines and the numbers of students that they have supervised to completion at doctoral level, to enable some exploration of the numbers of students that a supervisor might manage at that level.

A few core questions were asked of each interviewee in semi-structured interviews, and then there were follow-up probes and a section of questions theorising with the interviewee (Cousin 2009). The initial questions evolved after a pilot and included:

1   What have your experiences been of teaching students to research?
2   What have you found successful?
3   What have you found difficult?
4   How many students have you supervised?
5   What have they gone on to do?
6   What were you first conscious of when working with postgraduates?
7   How has that changed?

The probes included checking for salience by asking if the respondent felt a point was a widely held view, and some hypothetical questions relating discipline to pedagogy. Hesitations and ambiguities were followed up and each interviewee had a copy of their transcript to check before it was analysed.

Focus groups and interviews have been held with postgraduate students and analysed in a similar manner. Participants in conference discussions, at workshops on teaching and learning and on supervision development programmes have also contributed enormously to the evolution of this book.

All the academics interviewed were recommended as 'excellent' either by colleagues or by students, and sometimes by both. The interviews were all recorded and transcribed. The transcripts were initially coded and analysed into themes whilst looking for underlying concepts. Eventually the data settled into five areas which were united by an over-arching tension for the academics between the professional and the personal self.

The transcripts were then coded in several ways. Initially themes were created from the data (which led to the framework), and then statements were abstracted in relationship to certain questions (such as 'independence' and 'creativity') and compared with each other.

Stage 2: questionnaires

Workshops with academics were held in five research-led universities in the UK and Scandinavia, where the participants were asked to rate each approach on a Likert scale for

- importance to their practice (salience)
- how much they used an approach in their practice (espoused theory and theory-in-use, Argyris & Schon 1974)
- how much they would like to be skilled in a particular approach (development opportunities).

Fifty-five questionnaires were analysed; confidentiality and anonymity were assured. These questionnaires were designed to enable comparison of approach to supervision by discipline.

To assess whether the data is internally consistent as a whole and whether each approach is also internally consistent, it was entered into SPSS and the Cronbach's alpha reliability score over 15 items was 0.775. Cronbach's alpha was also run for each approach and four out of five of them were acceptable. The functional items scored 0.156. This is a very low score for reliability and may be explained by the fact that the functional approach is seen by some as a management or political tool, so for example, they may use this approach but not value it (an observation born out by reactions in several of the workshops exploring this framework). The other Cronbach's alpha scores were: enculturation – 0.717; critical thinking – 0.547; emancipation – 0.833 and quality of relationship – 0.685.

Small sample numbers mean that we cannot generalise about disciplinary differences, but if the results were replicated on a larger sample we could suggest that (after a workshop) supervisors can differentiate between the approaches and those from the hard pure subject groups might respond more readily to development opportunities that emphasised critical thinking, enculturation and quality of relationship approaches.

Stage 3: interactive poster session

An opportunistic sample of 35 academics was invited to see if there is any relationship between discipline, conceptions of knowledge and approaches to supervision. The academics were attending a teaching and learning event and were asked to volunteer to identify their discipline in terms of hard, soft, pure and applied (see below). They identified their preferred approaches to supervision by using different coloured stickers on posters. This was a public act and we would need further investigation to check whether that distorted the findings. There was an opportunity for academics to contribute new and different perceptions outside those proposed by Biglan and from the original research.

Two of the academics found it difficult to identify their discipline in Biglan's terms. However, they did accept that their work spanned two of the categories and were content to participate providing their contributions could be 'double-counted'.

Supervisors in the 'hard' subjects showed a slightly greater preference for functional and enculturation approaches and the 'soft' subjects showed a slightly greater preference for relationship development (see Figure 2.3). A more extensive study could be undertaken to ascertain whether or not this was statistically significant.

The discussions around the poster were very interesting. In the interviews supervisors had described many behaviours that were allocated to 'enculturation'. There was obviously some difficulty with that word for supervisors who encountered it first on a poster; they either asked what the definition of the word meant, and/or they withdrew from accepting the notion of power and direction that it implies. One US scientist said that over time he found that he had changed his mind, he had originally been very keen on 'enculturation' but now accepted that his students were still using the methods they had learned as scientists even if they went into consultancy.

The data so far suggests that there may be some differences in preferred approach to supervision between hard and soft subjects and between soft and applied subjects, but there is also considerable overlap. Further research is required to explore this and at this stage it is too early to look for much consistency between the different research methods.

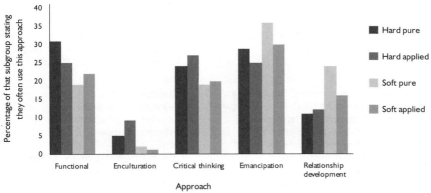

Figure 2.3 Supervisor's preference by subject characteristics

As a method of consultation and a vehicle for encouraging debate amongst busy academics who might not otherwise have been included, this was very successful.

Stage 4: workshops

Workshops have now been held for groups of between 10 and 60 academics at research-led universities in the UK, Sweden, Denmark, Estonia and at European and international conferences, where groups of academics have used this framework to explore how to resolve supervision and teaching dilemmas. Subsequent interviews and correspondence with some of these academics demonstrate that using the framework in this way can have a powerful illuminative effect and give the academic much greater self-confidence in their ability to resolve some of these dilemmas. The dilemmas that are discussed in these sessions are typically those addressed in Chapter 8.

To look for disciplinary differences, I adapted the two-dimensional model of subject characteristics proposed by Biglan (see Table 2.1) and discussed by Becher and Trowler (2001). Some subjects are in transition across disciplinary boundaries and 'double counting' was used to reflect this. The table has been adapted because some subjects have changed their emphasis, for example economics has become increasingly mathematical and so econometrics has been included in the 'hard applied' category.

Table 2.1 The relationships between subject matter characteristics and the structure and output of university departments (adapted from Biglan 1973a and 1973b)

	HARD Similar paradigm for content and research methods. More co-authors, more influences on research. Subjects more physical. Reality is more objective.	SOFT Similar paradigm for content and research methods. Research more independent. Subjects more relative/relational. Reality is more subjective.
PURE	Biochemistry, Botany, Chemistry, Maths, Microbiology, Physics, Physiology	Dance, English, Languages, Linguistics, Political science, Philosophy, Psychology, Sociology, Theology, Translation, Music
APPLIED *More time spent on service activities*	Econometrics, Engineering (inc Chemical, Civil, Structural, Electronic, Materials etc), Computer science, Environmental science, Food and nutrition, Medicine, Space technology	Business Studies, Accounting, Finance, Economics, Education, Educational development, Law, Management (inc Tourism, Retail, & Hospitality), Nursing and Health Care

All the quotes from supervisors in this text are allocated to one of these quadrants to preserve their anonymity and to enable comparison across disciplines. One of the themes that emerges from this analysis is that there is less difference between the disciplines when we examine research supervision than is suggested by previous authors who have examined pedagogies in the disciplines (Becher & Trowler 1989). The supervisors interviewed for this work gave clear examples of a functional approach regardless of whether they were engineers or educationalists, both they and the philosophers and pure scientists could all give examples of each approach. No one supervisor gave examples of every approach but when we took all the interviews together, each disciplinary group did.

The researcher's background

No qualitative study should ignore the researcher's background, and some readers might want to know that I have a background in psychology but have also always had an interest in economics. I see the social-psychological and economic factors as key drivers in our economy. Professionally I have worked in a range of public and private sector organisations, been a Headmistress and run my own consultancy, before moving into academia. My own PhD was undertaken in a Department of Educational Studies, but looked at conflict around medical doctors in general practice, and included a stimulating eclectic research methods programme. I had a new supervisor allocated to me half way through my research, so I have sympathy with that predicament, and I had a wonderful peer group of research students to work with. I have an equal passion for research and for teaching and most (but not all) of my postgraduate students have been very successful. My regret has always been that I did not study philosophy as an undergraduate, and this may explain why the strand 'critical thinking' has been of great interest to me.

Some readers might want to know if this framework flows from a cognitive or phenomenographic perspective (Åkerlind 2008). Åkerlind argues that two key perspectives are the cognitive constructivist where the objective is conceptual change and it assumes that different conceptions are independent of each other, whereas the phenomenographic constitutionalist perspective sees different conceptions related in a hierarchy of inclusiveness and its objective is conceptual expansion. I argue that this framework facilitates a growing awareness of the range of approaches that the academic can take to supporting the student doing research. Perhaps its strength is that it enables aspects of both perspectives to be used, for example the academic can use it to *compare and contrast* their approaches and *expand* awareness of the range of approaches available.

Using the framework to support compare and contrast, and expanding awareness

A typical academic development programme using this framework might ask the participant to:

1   Identify their own strengths as a supervisor of students doing research
2   Compare these with other colleagues
3   Interview students to find out what could support their learning at different stages of the research process
4   Compare these with the theories of supervision currently available
5   Describe the institutional, departmental and disciplinary norms for supervising research at different levels of higher education
6   Analyse and evaluate the power of various milestones
7   Hypothesise a range of ways in which the power of groups and disciplinary communities might be harnessed to support students doing research
8   Critically investigate the 'habitas' that the student will be engaged with
9   Critically reflect on the answers to No 3 in the light of learning theories (such as threshold concepts, transformative learning, learning taxonomies, identity formation)
10 Describe how their relationship with students begins, develops over time and their reaction to the different stages.

Adapted from journal entries described by Åkerlind (2008)

The research behind this book could be described as positivist because it does create a framework. As we have seen it is not the only framework possible and the boundaries are permeable, but many academics have found it useful when analysing their own practice and when trying to increase the options they have when confronted by perplexing situations with students.

There is a political undercurrent to this book; the increasing pressure to have larger numbers of students at postgraduate level and for research students to complete their studies within a limited time is encouraging performativity, compliance with institutional norms and instrumentality. Interestingly there is a counter movement coming originally from several centres for excellence in teaching and learning (CETLs) in the UK where there is encouragement to introduce research into the curriculum, but this provides a challenge to consistent assessment practices. I believe that an over-emphasis on the functional approach, to the exclusion of all others, creates a rigid and arid experience for both academic and student, so the introduction of four other approaches to working with research students is a deliberate attempt to put the functional approach in its rightful place. New academics need to master the functional skills, and this book does encourage that because if they do not they may never feel comfortable using the other approaches, but after that they need to be encouraged to look at how they teach and the core values they are espousing in a more critical manner.

In this chapter I have reviewed some of the alternative models that have been provided for looking at research supervision – most of them focusing on doctoral supervision. I have made the research behind this framework as clear as possible – it used a multimethod but largely qualitative approach, and included some less usual, but illuminating, ways of testing the data. In the next five chapters I explore each approach in more detail.

Further reading

Gatfield, T. J. (2005) 'An investigation into PhD supervisory management styles: Development of a dynamic conceptual model and its managerial implications'. *Journal of Higher Education Policy and Management.* 27.3: 311–325.

Grant, B. M. (2008) 'Agonistic struggle: Master–slave dialogues in humanities supervision'. *Arts and Humanities in Higher Education.* 7.1: 9–27.

Lee, A. and Green, B. (2009) 'Supervision as metaphor'. *Studies in Higher Education.* 34.6: 615–630.

Murphy, N., Bain, J., and Conrad, L. (2007) 'Orientations to Higher Degree Supervision'. *Higher Education.* 53: 209–234.

Chapter 3

Functional teaching and supervision

The functional approach: an introduction

In designing and delivering taught programmes, the functional approach is usually very much at the forefront of the programme leader's mind, not least because of the institutional procedures for quality assurance. The deadlines are clear, the procedures for ensuring access to information and study support will have been examined through validation and other quality assurance measures and increasingly the type and frequency of feedback given to students has become more prescribed as a result of league table pressures. In working with research students, however, particularly at doctoral level, these processes are not always so formulated, and there is some evidence from the interviews to suggest that it is the experienced research supervisors who recognise the advantages of structure even when working at this level. The academic who foregrounds this approach is aware of all of the procedures and timetables that need to be followed and keeps appropriate records. The student will understand clearly what is expected of them after every meeting and meetings will be regularly arranged. The roles of co-supervisors will also be made explicit and one supervisor will have the responsibility for identifying a series of milestones that keep the project on track, will agree a project plan with the student and monitor progress. The functional supervisor and the student are both clear about the assessment criteria that are going to be applied for examining, and the requirements for ethical practices are made explicit.

The functional approach also emerges in a series of guides to effective supervision (Wisker 2005, Eley & Jennings 2005, Taylor & Beasley 2005). An excellent companion guide to the functional approach to doctoral supervision is provided by Adrian Eley and Rowena Murray in *How to be an Effective Supervisor* (2009). They take the institutional approach and identify 27 different responsibilities that the institution has in ensuring effective supervision, each of these precepts (taken from the QAA 2004 code of practice) has an implication for policy and for supervisor training and development. They cover issues such as academic standards, regulations, admissions, responsibilities, communication, monitoring, support and feedback, assessment and appeals.

All these guides provide useful lists of tasks and vignettes of different situations, but they do not give academics a conceptual model to use in reflecting upon their beliefs about what supervising research students is about. A managerial approach to supervision is described by Vilkinas (2002), in which she applies a four-quadrant model with two dimensions (flexibility/stability and internal/external focus) to analysing supervisory tasks.

Stages that lend themselves to a functional approach to research supervision can include (not always in this order):

- Obtaining funding and resources
- Recruitment of students
- Induction
- Arranging co-supervision
- Arranging appropriate research methods training
- Clarifying expectations about roles, numbers and length of meetings
- Agreeing project management plans
- Timetabling plans for applications for ethical approval
- Record keeping and preparing relevant material for exam and/or postgraduate research boards
- Transfer arrangements from M Phil to PhD (most commonly known as an 'upgrade' or PhD confirmation). This is the most common route to a PhD in the UK
- Agreeing deadlines for drafting and submitting formative, summative assessed or publishable material
- Finding suitable internal and/or external examiners.

Eley and Murray (2009) also suggest checklists for what supervisors should know (p. 51) and of the documentation that they should ensure they have access to (p. 52).

Managing research as a project

The functional approach to research supervision is most closely associated with a managerial approach. Experience was mentioned earlier as sometimes leading to greater use of the functional approach but it is not the only impetus, there are national and international influences: the pressure internationally from governments and funding bodies to improve completion rates has led to a focus on the processes or stages of supervision (Neumann 2007, Park 2007). Neumann refers to a change in supervisory style becoming 'noticeable in some humanities faculties where the move was towards a science model for supervision' (2007: 466). In the UK the focus on a skills for employability agenda (Roberts Review 2002) highlighted the need for doctoral students (and subsequently for contract researchers) to develop and maintain generic skills which are intended to enhance their employability.

Universities are the link between many (sometimes conflicting) bodies and the research students. They have to meet the quality demands that the institutional audit process will make (via the Quality Assurance Agency (QAA) in the UK), and they will also provide the appeal mechanism in the event of any dispute between the student and academics or examiners. These lead to the need for more extensive documentation than used to be required in the past. Funding bodies also have their own requirements: in the UK the Higher Education Funding Council and the Research Councils have become more concerned about time to completion for doctoral students and make demands about research methods training. Governments have a stake in what they see as one of the engines of the 'knowledge economy' and international bodies (especially the European Community) are interested in harmonisation so that there is some comparability in standards across nations. Considerable funding also comes from charitable bodies (in the UK the Wellcome Trust is a good example) and they too have agendas and priorities to be met. Employers and professional bodies may have very specific requirements, and the academic may need to navigate carefully through a maze of commercial issues and demands, however commercial organisations are sometimes more willing to be flexible than we expect.

All of these demands mean that there has to be some institutional structure to the supervision process. A supervisor who has been awarded a large grant (for that discipline) and who now has a considerable research team said:

> We have agendas for supervision meetings planned for a year ahead. I have got separate folders with all their stuff in, I have an admin assistant so that it is all filed properly and (I know what date literature reviews etc. are due). I keep documentary evidence and follow up if they don't write about what we have agreed. We have a fortnightly PhD seminar series where we all (supervisors and researchers) contribute ... yes, there is an awful lot of structure and this is a relatively new unit so I am setting the tone and values for it. I have got other bids in which mean that new PhD students will come into an existing culture. (Soft applied)

This emphasis on negotiated (rather than imposed) agreement was described by a senior supervisor with experience of working both in the UK and the USA:

> Every meeting I used to have we used to write up notes and I would get the student to sign them as well as myself and I would give them a copy. So the idea was that we had a common understanding of what we talked about. We did annual reports. At the end of the first year annual report they were assessed in that with an independent examiner, usually

from completely outside of the field so that this didn't necessarily reflect special expertise and therefore a bias here. (Hard applied)

This supervisor continued to describe another procedure that has been used across the disciplines – that of keeping log books. In the soft disciplines they can be used as reflective diaries, but the rationale in all subject groups is the same – to encourage metacognitive thinking. Another underlying theme from both of these supervisors was the need to establish a pattern and structure early on in the process – their argument was that once it was established it would begin to maintain itself and support momentum.

> ... we also insisted they kept log books, which from time to time we would sign off on. Most of the formalities were really only needed in the first year to 18 months, because after that students had adopted a practice that was so well based I'm sure they probably still do it today. It's the sort of thing you learn, (as a supervisor) I think, the need to have very regular meetings early on. (Hard applied)

Another academic described how their use of the functional approach gave the student security when the co-supervisor was rather chaotic:

> There were some really bad practices going on but I didn't get involved in any of that ... (the other supervisor) would call the student down and then leave her sitting outside for an hour because he was busy, and then ask her what she wanted, he having requested the meeting in the first place. ... I just modelled what I thought were good practices which were around discussing what we were going to do, asking for things a week ahead so I could read them, giving feedback when I said I would, or if I could not do it, saying when it would be ready ... (Soft applied)

The functional approach can be used to help the student to focus, in this case the academic is talking about a student who was rushing their work and producing a large amount of unfocused material that had many errors:

> We started to use words about 'slowing down' and only writing two hundred words a day (rather than 2,000 words). I would say to her 'I want two hundred words of good stuff' or 'we don't want any other chapters, we just want this chapter revamped, we don't want to see anything else and if you send it to us we will send it back unread'. It became very directive because she was not hearing what we said. We met about every four months. We used a whole range of other structural techniques as well, including recording agreements, her talking into the computer rather than writing. It worked, it was astonishing. (Soft applied)

Funding for research students

At an undergraduate level introducing research into the curriculum may require negotiation with validation and accreditation bodies. The first stage at any level is usually to confirm that funding is available, both for the student and the resources that may be required. Some postgraduate students are recruited as part of a wider grant application, some are funded from university funds and many research councils now offer studentships as three- or four-year doctoral training grants. These mixed funding sources can lead to some complicated algorithms when it comes to working out how many doctoral students can be recruited each year and it is possible to use grant funding to create even more posts. An example of this leverage is demonstrated by the Engineering and Physical Sciences Research Council (EPSRC) awarding funding of £24m to Oxford University for a Doctoral Training Centre (DTC); the university managed to raise a further £12.5m from other sources and only 90 out of 148 students were funded directly through DTC grants (see http://www.ukcge.ac.uk/events/pastevents/0809area/sc09.htm).

Recruiting the right student(s)

Time spent on recruitment is an investment in a more problem-free future, and this is a necessity at the doctoral level. Professor Eric Mazur, a physicist at Harvard who has also researched and published extensively on pedagogical matters, described how he involves his whole team in his recruitment process (Lee 2008b: 25) and he says he makes no discrimination in the procedures to follow between taking on a PhD student and any other member of staff.

If Eric Mazur is right about the need for all members of the team to be involved in and committed to the decision to take on a new student, it requires a level of advance planning within a department. This may be a counsel of perfection, but the closer we can move towards each member of the academic team being involved in the recruitment process from the beginning, the easier it will probably be in the long term.

Another vital part of the recruitment process is usually to begin discussions about the research project. The effective academic will have some idea of the resources necessary, the availability and accessibility of data. Taking on a student and then discussing what they are going to do for their research has happened more in the sciences than in arts and humanities; it arises where academics have funding for large projects and they may not have decided how to divide up the work that needs to be done when a new research student starts. Increasingly all funders (both arts and sciences) prefer to award fewer, larger sums; this effectively devolves the management of these funds to the academic. In these circumstances identifying the student who will have a passion for enquiry before they start with you becomes more important; students with prescribed research projects can have difficulty in maintaining momentum during any difficult periods that arise in the future.

> There is a university policy about recruitment, so I have to put an advert out along the themes of the bid. I ask them to send in a proposal to say how they would go about one of the themes and then they come in and do a ten-minute Powerpoint presentation and we ask them questions about the paper they have sent in advance ... (Soft applied)

Even when recruitment is carefully undertaken there can be problems:

> I recruited a prize-winning first class honours student. She looked an absolutely red hot character. It was evident, even from early on in the supervision, that she wasn't simulating new ideas of her own, she wasn't asking questions. In other words, if I gave her something to look at she came back with a very complete piece of work but there was no originality and no challenge in what was emerging. I've always had a very candid relationship with my students so in the end I said 'I don't think things are going so well'. And she said 'No I feel that as well'. I asked her: 'So why do you feel this is?' She said 'I don't feel motivated about it' and her skills set just wasn't well matched to research ... she went on to be very successful (in business life) and she is happy, she was with me for four or five months and that was probably one of the most rapid fallouts. And even though I was meeting her every day to try and provide her with support (that for me is a very intensive support) there was no acrimony about it. I think we both recognised this just wasn't for her.
>
> It's interesting because she was such a bright capable person at an undergraduate level. To have a mis-match like that, I've never come across before. (Hard applied)

There is another radical humanist view of recruitment which could set the supervisor in collision with organisational pressures to complete. This supervisor described this view:

> that everybody should have a chance and you don't know their potential until they try ... this is a liberal education at its best and of course the ethos of a liberal education is that it is the journey that counts and if you (the student) are not going to submit your thesis for an award that is all right. (Soft pure)

Some students and academic colleagues will have what they feel is a philosophical objection to the functional approach, and it may be coming from this radical humanist position. Resolving this conflict can be difficult and it is symbolic of wider conflicts between managerialism and collegiality which can arise in universities.

The recruitment process is a two-way selection process. The student also deserves the opportunity of getting to know key staff and the department before they commit a considerable amount of their life and money to working with you, and an interview alone may not have given them sufficient information.

How many research students should an academic have?

The answer to this depends on the organisation of the academic team, the nature of the research, other academic commitments and the amount of funding available. Some universities have clear workload models which include supervision as a teaching activity. At masters level there may be quite large cohorts of research students where the requirements for a dissertation are less strenuous, but students need to be made aware of how much supervision time is available for them so that they can plan ahead. The student who knows from the beginning of their dissertation that they only have three or four supervision sessions is more likely to be focused. At an undergraduate level research on individual projects can be demanding of academic time, and this is part of the reason for introducing group projects.

There are outstanding supervisors who have large numbers of doctoral students at one time (up to 15 or more), but they are exceptional and often have exceptional resources. They have also learned how to include students and post-doctoral researchers as collaborators in the academic team, so that they support each other's learning. Frequently universities would get concerned if a supervisor had more than six doctoral students because they would suspect that the students could not receive the level of attention that would be reasonable. The number of students an academic can have will depend ultimately on the allocation of resources that they have at their disposal – especially both their own and others' time. Where an academic is using post-doctoral students and more junior academics as supervisors, they may need to spend more time mentoring, monitoring and tutoring supervisors than they do actually supervising students.

Table 3.1 shows the disciplines and groupings of 20 of the supervisors interviewed and the numbers of doctoral students that they have supervised. Even when we take into account the fact that the table includes supervisors who have very different lengths of service (from 8 to 30 years), it is obvious that it is in the hard and applied subjects that larger numbers are being supervised at any one time. This may be a reflection of the funding available – the configuration of the research councils demonstrates that they are keen to support research where there is an element of knowledge transfer.

Table 3.1 Some of the supervisors interviewed and their numbers of doctoral students

Subject	Hard/soft Pure/applied	No of research students supervised to completion
Bioscience	HP	30
Physics	HP	15
Physics	HP	40
Physics	HP	50+
Psychology	SA	14
Management	SA	3
Sociology	SA	5
Economics	SA	8
Politics	SA	50
Psychology	SA	7
Management	SA	12
Engineering	HA	7
Engineering	HA	18
Computing	HA	3
Engineering	HA	100
Engineering	HA	50
Engineering	HA	20
Philosophy	SP	25
Philosophy	SP	15
Arts	SP	10

Who can be included in a team supervising research students?

Various codes of practice emphasise that the primary supervisor must have had experience of co-supervision before taking on a doctoral student of their own. This means that at least, most students have two supervisors. It is my contention that there is a much wider network of support for the student to draw from and the academic needs to be aware of it (Lee 2008b). This section introduces some definitions of terms that will be used throughout the book and may suggest roles that have not yet been considered in your institution. The principal or primary supervisor is accountable for ensuring that the institution meets its obligations to the student, but they may delegate some of these responsibilities. The secondary supervisor may be an 'apprentice' mostly observing the process for the first time, or they may have specific expertise which the student is going to need a great deal of. Sometimes students will have work-based or industrial supervisors and universities need to consider what training or development these people need as well. Occasionally there are issues of commercial confidentiality in some research projects, and the parameters surrounding these need to be explored in advance. Advisers can either be appointed or they can emerge more informally as the research progresses. They usually have a supportive role and may help with a mathematical or technical aspect of the work, they may be graduate teaching assistants or post-doctoral researchers in the department and their closeness to the student world can be very helpful for research students seeking help. The peer group of students is very important in the social construction of learning and for providing a feeling of belonging.

> When the students first arrived we had a two-day workshop on philosophy and methodology for the whole team, so all the academics involved contributed and knew all the students. (Soft applied)

Other members of the academic team who need to be included are the librarians and postgraduate administrators – these are key people, sometimes ignored, yet they can make all the difference to a student submitting successfully and on time.

Students need to find out who the postgraduate teaching co-ordinator is; if they want to pursue a teaching career gaining some experience (and financial reward) can be helpful. There can be opportunities for experienced students to add to their qualifications; in the UK some universities offer a course of study leading to an Associate Fellowship of the Higher Education Academy (AFHEA). Graduate teaching assistants benefit from teaching opportunities in many ways: they learn the subject, enhance their CV, become more familiar with the tacit culture of the academic and disciplinary world (Eraut 2007) and gain income. The main disadvantage is the time that it takes away from research because they need preparation both to teach the subject and in how to teach (Lee & Pettigrove 2010).

Other members of the university or college team are also key to the student experience, but are often not recognised as such: the people organising transferable skills training, departmental co-ordinators of teaching assistants, the careers and library services, student counselling and financial advice centres, the student union postgraduate representative and the housing officers. As one student said in a focus group:

I have just heard today that I am going to have to leave my flat, I was promised it for the whole duration of my programme. How can I even think about my research with this hanging over me? (Law Student)

Often service providers are unaware of the impact they can have on research students. These service providers can be a small or invisible section of the university and it is wise to brief them and raise the profile of postgraduate research students (Lee 2008b).

Arranging relevant induction and training for the research student

As in any other form of employment, the first days of work will set the student's expectations for the future. Introducing the student to fellow academics and students is a key function for the supervisor to accomplish as soon as possible. Some departments are organised to provide research methods training for a cohort of students over the first couple of terms; many supervisors insist on acceptable IT skills, database and reference management before the student begins to research, and the generic skills training now provided in many UK universities also needs to be organised. At the very least, producing some recommended reading will tell the research student that their supervisor is interested in their existence even when most of the student's initial time is committed elsewhere. Eley and Murray (2009) list some key elements that need to be covered in inducting postgraduate students (p. 90) and report that students requested that they be encouraged to ask even 'silly' questions. They also emphasise the need for the academic to use the induction period to assess the student and the type of supervision that they will most benefit from.

Keeping records

Institutions will do this differently but there will normally be three forms of records which all need to be kept to maintain an audit trail, but which also guide and support good practice in supervision:

- University records
- Faculty/school/departmental/college records
- Academic/supervisor's records.

There will be some form of project approval procedure. This will name the primary supervisor and any external collaborators. It may enquire into the academic's workload and resources and ask for a short project description. At a doctoral level it will require the signature of senior figures from within the university before the student can register.

In the UK most doctoral students register for an M Phil and subsequently apply for transfer to PhD status (the most common exception to this process is when applying to undertake a PhD by submitting already published works). There will also be a university pro-forma for confirming transfer from M Phil to PhD, but the process that this entails can differ. In some cases students have to write certain draft chapters of their thesis (typically a literature review or methodology section), in other cases students are asked to make a presentation and write a paper about their project so far.

The records that are kept more locally are often six- or twelve-monthly annual reviews. In some cases departments meet annually to review the progress of all of their postgraduate students and these reviews are key to that process. It is good practice for these reviews to include an overview of the project and its progress so far, training and personal development planning needs for the student and documentation of any problems (suffered by either the student or the academic). The student should contribute a written section outlining what support they have had and what support they think they may need in the future. Both the university and the more local records may be required for University Research Committees or for Postgraduate Schools monitoring purposes.

Keeping records of meetings between academic and student can be difficult, for example if they are meeting in the laboratory all the time. However, some structure needs to be in place to record some more formal meetings, which may be every few months. I use a pro-forma which simply identifies the areas discussed, the objectives that the students are going to work on next, any resources, training or introductions that I am going to provide and the date of the next meeting. The student or I complete the form at the end of the meeting and we both sign and keep a copy of it. These can be important pieces of paper in the event of any later disputes.

Managing the transfer status

In the UK the formal transfer from M Phil to a doctoral programme is a useful milestone for doctoral research, at other levels a similar function can be achieved by setting a deadline for the submission of a formatively assessed piece of work. Whilst the process by which transfer is granted will be a locally determined one, the academic can usefully use the process as a signpost to keep the student on track. At this stage a student who finds this process intellectually difficult might be better guided to transfer on to a different programme rather than encounter insuperable problems at the viva. Providing this discussion is tactfully handled, it can be a relief to the student who is feeling incapable of achieving the level of work required.

Supervisors are aware of the need for help over the transfer process:

I try to give clear guidelines for transfer reports, the more clear guidelines
I can give the better. (Hard applied)

As in any assessment procedure, there may be mitigating circumstances
which need to be taken into account, so lack of intellectual capability needs
to be separated from emotional or practical problems which time may resolve.

Submission of the research

At an undergraduate level there are a variety of assessment methods available
including presentations, posters and project reports. At masters level, some
supervisors find it difficult to mark dissertations that they have been closely
involved in, so double marking (preferably double-blind marking) rather
than just moderation is helpful here.

At doctoral level the selection of the examiners (internal and external)
should be discussed between the student and academic in good time. Around
the world there are a variety of procedures, for example in Australia examiners
independently provide written reports, in many European countries there is
a public defence but in the UK there is a viva voce examination held in
private. If the examination is held in private there is an increasing likelihood
that university procedures will require the appointment of an independent
chairperson (although that chairperson is sometimes replaced by a tape-
recorder!). The supervisor needs to decide whether they want to be in the
viva or not, but if they are they need to warn the student that they are merely
there as an observer and any contributions they make must be limited to
points of clarification only. Otherwise the student may be disappointed with
a perceived lack of support from a hitherto friendly and accessible supervisor.

The examiners must understand the context and methods used in the
research; they must be able to give reasonable time to the examination
process. The student, supervisors and examiners must be alert to and openly
declare any possible conflicts of interest – and in a small research field this is
quite possible.

The student needs to be prepared for their viva, the chapter on critical
thinking can alert them to some of the questions that they are likely to be asked.
Murray (2009) provides a particularly clear guide to demystifying the enigma
that is the viva (p. 3) and gives advice about how to handle the wide range
of questions that the examiners can produce – although it is aimed primarily
at students this is also a useful text for academics preparing to conduct oral
examinations. Jackson and Tinkler (2007) and Tinkler and Jackson (2004)
have also written useful guides on the doctoral examination process. It is
helpful if the student is aware of what the examiners will be looking for and
these authors identify the main purposes of the viva as: ensuring authenticity;
placing research in a wider context; assessing understanding; clarifying any

weaknesses; defending the approach, methods and conclusions; deciding outcome; maintaining consistent standards and testing oral skills.

Trafford and Leshem (2008) suggest that doctorateness is demonstrated by combining a high level of innovation and development, with a high level of scholarship and interpretation. The sorts of questions that illuminate this quadrant are below.

Can the student:

1   Defend doctorateness
2   Critique and analyse
3   Conceptualise findings
4   Develop conceptual frameworks
5   Synthesise concepts
6   Establish links/concepts
7   Design research and operational fieldwork?

These are not the *only* questions to be covered in the assessment, but Trafford and Leshem argue that they are typical of the questions which distinguish what they call 'doctorateness' from other research.

Box 3.1 identifies the key stages in the research supervision process, when looking at it from a functional perspective.

Academics are aware of the need to implement the functional approach with sensitivity:

> I have seen the advantage of structure. In most cases it means giving deadlines, word length, sources, suggested topics. But it does depend

---

Box 3.1 Summary of key stages in the research supervision process

1   Ensuring funds, academic time and resources are available
2   Recruiting the student
3   Recruiting and organising the academic team
4   Arranging relevant induction and training for the student
5   Regular written reports of meetings for university monitoring
6   Extension request if required
7   Submission of project/dissertation/thesis
8   Marking and exam board procedures

In addition, for doctoral supervision
9   Transfer from M Phil to PhD status procedures completed (where appropriate)
10 Arrangement of external examiners

on the student. Sometimes I would allow much more freedom. (Soft applied)

Some project management tools: Gantt charts, critical path analysis

Some research students fail simply because of bad planning. There are a range of project management tools which help to identify key tasks, what resources are needed and when, if target completion dates are to be met.

Simple flow charts should not be ignored as a tool for working out the order in which tasks need to be undertaken. The first guideline is to identify the end date for the project and work backwards. However, most projects require students to be carrying out more than one task at a time, so a Gantt chart might be an appropriate tool.

A Gantt chart is a spreadsheet showing all the tasks with their start and finish dates on a time line; it is named after Henry Gantt, an American engineer. They are often used in funding bids as a diagrammatic representation of the plan to convince grant givers that a project is achievable.

Critical path analysis (CPA) is a slightly more sophisticated tool for identifying those tasks which, if completed late, will cause the whole project to be late. Once these tasks have been identified then it is obvious to give them the highest priority. A complete CPA would enable the researcher to calculate the shortest possible route to completion.

Risk management techniques are also useful. This is often achieved by creating a table which lists all possible risks to the project, identifies the likelihood and priority of each risk and a strategy for dealing with it should it arise (see Table 3.2).

Whatever form of project management is used, it is important to build in considerable contingency time. The results may not come back as expected, key data sources may not be available, the researcher might be offered some teaching that they want to do, there can be funding or personal problems. Different problems may require different periods of time as contingencies (Burke 2005) and it may not be excessive if they amount to allowing a contingency time of 30–50 per cent. Box 3.2 takes a functional approach to listing the quality assurance and administrative questions that the academic needs to be able to answer for their own institution.

Table 3.2 Outline of a table that can be used to analyse risk

Description of potential failure	Importance	Likelihood of failure	Recommended action	Person responsible

Ethical matters

This section focuses more on procedures around ethics in research. In Chapter 7 there is further discussion of ethical issues around boundaries and the relationship between the academic and the student doing research. In practice ethical questions arise in each part of the framework (for example: how ethical is it to encourage a limited approach through enculturation or to allow failure if following an emancipatory approach?) and each discipline has its own ethical challenges. In the West, ethical study arose originally from the 'three wise men' of Socrates, Plato and Aristotle. It is now recognised as pervading every discipline, every type of employment and as being a vital factor in research. There are three aspects of the work with students doing research that need some examination: firstly the relationship between student and academic, secondly the research itself and thirdly the links between ethics and employability. In this section we look particularly at preparing for the scrutiny that ethical committees provide and make some comment on the ethics involved in joint publishing, but it is important to realise that no one ethical perspective has the monopoly of wisdom, and true ethical thinking includes weighing up many perspectives.

Most students at a postgraduate level now have to obtain ethical approval from their own departmental or university ethics committees before they can

---

Box 3.2 Self assessment questions about administrative procedures

Key administrative questions underpinning the functional approach
   In your institution what are the:

- minimum and maximum periods of study and registration procedures
- minimum reporting procedures and times
- procedures for appointing supervisors and co-supervisors
- relevant level descriptors
- taught courses that might be useful for your student
- assessment procedures, submission, examination procedures and timetable
- procedures for dealing with illness, disability, plagiarism, parental leave etc.
- amounts of time that the supervisor is expected to spend on a one-to-one basis with undergraduates, masters students and doctoral students, or roughly how often are they expected to meet
- and what is the appeal process in your institution?

commence their study. In some cases they also have to get ethical approval from an employer such as the NHS (National Health Service) or a professional body.

Students can often find completing ethical application forms a tedious process, and this is a point where they may need encouragement to keep going. In applying for ethical approval (sometimes now called by ethics committees merely 'an opinion') the student is not just completing regulatory paperwork, the whole protocol for the research can be developed and probably should be influenced by the questions addressed during the process. It is also an important process to begin early, because it can take time to get ethical approval and this can delay data collection. Sample participant information sheets and risk analysis charts that relate to your discipline can save students a great deal of time. If a study is well designed, there should be no problem in gaining ethical approval; completing the application will help the student work out some of the details of their study, and can save them time later on. If a body such as an NHS ethics committee grants approval, it is likely that the university will be able to fast-track an application through their own committee procedure.

Ethical decisions face the student at every twist and turn of their research. Good academics emphasise both duty ethics (e.g. how long do you think you need to keep your original data anonymised and secure for?) and normative ethics (e.g. what would the British Psychological Society's Code of Practice say about this breach of confidence?).

There can be no future for the researcher who creates misleading data for expediency, but the question for academics is where and how do we include ethical training in the research student's curriculum? If there is a recognised postgraduate training programme it may be addressed as part of this function; if the supervisor is relying upon enculturation to transmit ethical approaches, they may need to timetable specific discussions about it.

Ethical questions often arise when academics and students seek to publish together so it is better to discuss authorship and expectations of who will write which sections at an early stage. Some academics make it part of the induction procedure and include an explicit agreement that the student will not publish anything related to their research without discussing it first with their supervisor. Even making this requirement explicit raises its own ethical questions, but whatever agreement is reached, it should be recorded and the records updated if renegotiated. It is generally considered to be good practice if more senior academics are encouraged to give more junior colleagues opportunities to be first author when this is justified.

Academics do not need to be experts in all these issues (project management, curriculum design, administration and ethics) to be able to perform their role as a functional academic adequately, but they do need to know what needs to be done, where expertise lies and to take responsibility for ensuring that the right things happen for their students.

Box 3.3 Summary – the functional approach

Below are a series of suggestions that will help the academic identify the most essential elements of recruiting, teaching and supervising postgraduate students.

1   Actively recruit the best you can. Devise exercises to check the student can work at the required level, before they are accepted.
2   Organise an induction checklist which covers key places, key people (in department and in discipline) and encourages students to develop their own research subculture.
3   Have a discussion about expectations and roles – who is to be contacted for what and how.
4   Ensure each student has a realistic study plan that has dates by each element and arrange key meetings a year ahead.
5   Insert assessment exercises early in the curriculum to identify any students who will need additional help to complete.
6   Keep a record of meetings that the student completes. This record can include: subjects discussed, objectives to be met before the next meeting and date of next meeting. Both parties keep copies.
7   Hold regular seminars and conferences for students so they present their work to staff and each other.
8   Organise a research methods programme to introduce students to different methods and methodologies, good research practices, ethical issues and key researchers inside and outside the institution.
9   Devise writing exercises that are easier to give written feedback on – to help students to write at the right level.
10   Benchmark work against recognised norms. Introduce the assessment criteria early on in the programme and make frequent reference to them.
11   Include research students in academic life, for example inviting them to journal clubs, coffee meetings and enabling them to work as graduate teaching assistants.
12   Make sure that there is a clear point of contact for when problems arise (for both students and academics).
13   Make sure that there is a research supervisor's handbook available and regularly add information to update academics on any new procedures.
14   Hold departmental reviews of all postgraduate students' progress.

Box 3.3 summarises the most essential elements of recruiting, teaching and supervising postgraduate students.

In this chapter I have described elements of the functional approach, identifying some of the practices which experienced academics have found help their students towards completing research projects. There has been a movement towards various collective provisions of research training (Neumann 2003, Park 2007) and this chapter cites evidence that there is a movement towards the functional paradigm of supervision even across the soft disciplines. However, a functional approach on its own is insufficient, and the next chapters describe other approaches which need to be blended with it in order to create a holistic experience for students doing research.

Further reading

Eley, A. and Murray, R. (2009) *How to be an Effective Supervisor.* Maidenhead: Open University McGraw-Hill Education.

QAA (2004) *Code of Practice for the Assurance of Academic Quality and Standards in Higher Education. Section 1: Postgraduate research programmes.* http://www.qaa.ac.uk/academicinfrastructure/codeOfPractice/section1/postgrad2004.pdf accessed 29 November 2009.

Taylor, S. and Beasley, N. (2005) *A Handbook for Doctoral Supervisors.* Abingdon: Routledge.

Wisker, G. (2005) *The Good Supervisor.* Basingstoke: Macmillan.

Chapter 4

Supporting enculturation

The enculturation approach: an introduction

This refers to the process of socialisation or acculturalisation into the discipline, the working milieu (e.g. the academic department and the university) and the national culture. A person is 'enculturated' when they are comfortable being or working at all these levels. They have learned the traditional content of a culture and assimilated its practices and values. Their membership of the relevant groups is accepted and others may seek their advice on such matters. There are issues of acculturation into both the institution, the community of the discipline, the country/civilisation and epistemological access. It usually requires a long period of study and an ability to acquire the tacit knowledge required to become a fully functioning member of an academic community in any discipline.

Helping the student to belong

In this approach, learning is seen as developing within a societal context (Leonard 2001, Delamont, Atkinson & Parry 2000). From these writers we understand the importance of becoming a member of a discipline. Delamont *et al.* (2000) argued from empirical work that academics identify themselves by their discipline first and by their university and department second. There are also frequent references to an apprenticeship model in this context, so the research student needs to acquire a great deal of professional and interpersonal knowledge about how research and academic life is conducted here. This is subtle knowledge which is not explicitly taught but it is essential that the student learns it if they are to succeed and become a skilful practitioner.

Others have also noted that the student begins study by experiencing a form of 'legitimate peripheral participation' and is offered examples of mastery to reflect upon (Lave & Wenger 1991). The academic team can offer many opportunities for participation including leading seminars, attending conferences and undertaking teaching assistant activities.

The academic working from this approach at a doctoral level will prioritise the view that achieving a PhD is about becoming a member of an academic discipline (Leonard 2001: 98). Direction from the supervisor about both academic and behavioural matters may be more apparent here and as an apprentice, the student looks to the master to learn how to create a masterpiece.

The growing use of the term 'early stage researchers' (as agreed within the ten 'Salzburg principles' by the European Universities Association, EUA 2005) instead of 'doctoral students' is already in use. It emphasises that they are looking to develop people who will have a career in research, rather than people who will complete or crown their studies with a doctoral degree.

The academic may be a diagnostician, and like a family doctor, will provide some specific expertise as well as being a gatekeeper to many more learning resources, specialist opinions and networks. The academic can choose which gates to open, particularly in the early stages of the student or researcher's life. Within this understanding therefore, there is also an understanding of the power of the academic in its widest sense. Not only is the researcher 'present' (Brew 2001) in this approach, the academic is also 'present' as well.

There is another aspect of the power dynamic that arises from the academic being gatekeeper to the qualification and the academic discipline: that of ownership (or even suppression) of the final result. Original research can be dangerous in that it can undermine previously dearly held beliefs and careers. The struggle can be political on several levels. The student needs to be aware of how powerful (or not) their academic is in the institution. In the case of international students the academic is also gatekeeper to an even bigger issue: the cultural context in which the degree is being taken (Wisker 2005). There are opportunities for power games and argument about who 'owns' the research and subsequent conference presentations and publications.

Enculturation involves helping students to understand what constitutes academic writing and work in their disciplines through feedback and assessment. Students' performance in a range of writing tasks gives academics insights into students' conceptions of academic writing, identifies students' strengths and weaknesses in writing and helps academics to adjust their approach to writing to meet students' development needs. Through feedback, discussion of writing practices and outputs and assessment, students can develop their conceptions of writing.

Another aspect of enculturation is discourse literacy. This focuses on writing up – which is where many students state their difficulties arise. It includes pedagogical strategies to help the PhD student with project management, writing the literature review, skeleton sentences and creating the argument (Kamler & Thomson 2006).

Thow and Murray (2001) argue that the task of writing is often daunting for the research student because work is not produced on a sequential basis. They recommend visualising the structure of the project. The academic acts as facilitator, introducing a structured approach to writing and enabling students to adapt it to their projects. The discussions are academic-led but they are also dynamic, the student has to contribute and eventually own the work.

The dangers of apprenticeship were also highlighted by McWilliam and James (2002) 'Its pedagogy has been characterised by some – perhaps unfairly – as one in which the precocious few were called to emulate the master as scholar' (quoted in Taylor & Beasley 2005: 18).

Interviews with supervisors identified some of the ways in which the student is initially offered 'legitimate peripheral participation':

> I believe they need to get in the lab straight away, they learn more by doing practical work and then they will appreciate the literature. Initially I will suggest tasks and introduce them to the technical staff and lay out what I want done to get them started. (Hard pure)

> I give my book to all my students. (Hard applied)

> Students need to know what 'good enough' looks like. (Hard applied)

> I get them to do conference presentations and write proceedings, I go with them if they are presenting for the first time. (Soft applied)

The academic aims to move the student to a point of independence, the objective is a 'mutual engagement, joint enterprise and a shared repertoire' (Cousin & Deepwell 2005: 59):

> I ask: are they safe to be let loose on the community because technically those with a PhD are in charge of their own research? (Hard applied)

> I would feel I had failed if they did not stay in the field ... my students all know their academic grandfather. (Hard applied)

The failure to move to independence causes anxiety:

> The students you worry about are those who still turn to you in the viva looking for confirmation that they are OK. (Soft applied)

Breaking unspoken rules

In any environment there are tacit rules (Eraut 2007), which students need to learn to uncover if they really wish to belong:

> – there was actually someone who was a post doc who broke, you know, maybe rules that I had never formulated, because I don't formulate rules for that, but I consider them rules, which are ones of, you know, collaborative atmosphere rather than competitive atmosphere and ones

where you, where you share results and resources and, and you don't, for example, take other people's results and publish them separately. You know you have to respect some pretty strict rules about authorship for example, in my group and so, yes; I have (had that problem) ... and it upset many people in the group ... Probably the most important rule is everybody should be in line with the common good of the group; never put their own interest ahead of that of the group. (Hard pure)

This emphasis on teamwork raises both ethical and cultural questions. In the past an academic has frequently been an isolated researcher. Publishing scientific results to enable replication has been a major source of verification in the hard sciences, and maybe now we are seeing a cultural change which has implications for supervisor development. Later in the same interview this academic described how he had (reluctantly) arranged an expensive residential team-building workshop for his researchers, and how surprised he had been that his team had responded so positively to it.

Enculturation and ethics

Here a professor argues again for teamwork in the laboratory:

I think science is a very collaborative endeavour and ... there has to be an immaculate honesty in science and I have very, very high standards in that respect ... So in a sense this accountability in my group is, and high ethical standards, (are) ensured by the fact that we collaborate on everything ... And it's not just one person And you know whenever there is an incident of some, you know, unethical conduct, not in my group but anywhere, you read about it in newspapers sometimes, I always make a point of discussing that with my group ... And marvelling 'how in the world that was possible in a scientific enterprise which prides itself in honesty and transparency'. (Hard pure)

An ethical stance can be developed in many ways. The academic supervising students who research will (consciously or unconsciously) role model it, for example by emphasising the need for thoroughness, transparency and the consideration of alternative points of view and in the quotation above the academic is demonstrating an articulation of these values.

Developing an academic identity

The enculturation process is about the student developing an academic identity and it is assumed that the supervisor is central to that process for the research student. McAlpine *et al.* have studied the weekly logs of 20 Canadian education students. Each week students were asked to reflect on what the most significant event was that had contributed to their feeling of being an academic or belonging to an academic community. The results were as below, and writing or communicating was highly differentiated with 22 different codes:

> Writing or communicating
>> Thesis writing
>> Writing papers
>> Grant applications
>> Submitting journal articles or conference papers
>> Presenting at conferences
> Reading or knowing literature
>> Presenting at non-conference venues
>> Analysing data
>> Consulting
>> Peer modelling academic practice
>> Gaining approval for proposed research
>> Attending a conference
>> Meeting advisors/supervisors
>> Attending an oral defence
>> Finishing comprehensives
> Teaching,
> Service (membership of student committees, participation in departmental review and editing)
> Career development
>
> (McAlpine, Jazvac-Martek & Hopwood 2007)

Here writing emerges as an important skill. It may apply more to doctoral students who present mainly written theses, but it is an important area for the academic to examine. How much writing should the academic insist upon, how often and can it be shared with the cohort or are there concerns about confidentiality?

Enculturation in different disciplines

Murray (2006) encourages students to identify the different conventions of writing in the disciplines; she suggests that they explore language, how arguments are represented, how the researcher is represented, the structure revealed and the options for style and structure. The Carnegie Initiative on the Doctorate (CID) was a five-year programme, started in the USA in 2001. The first question it sought to address was 'what is the purpose of the doctorate?' and the answer they explored was 'stewardship of the disciplines'. They wanted to map and build these fields of knowledge and the project focused on six different disciplines to do this: chemistry, education, English, history, mathematics and neuroscience. These fields were deliberately chosen because they included new and old disciplines and demonstrated variation in a number of other different ways, e.g. different funding patterns, time-to-career, attrition rates, scope and structure of dissertation (Golde & Walker 2006). Essayists were invited to contribute thoughts on the best way of structuring doctoral education in their field. What follows are some examples of their contributions, but the complete texts are a valuable source and necessary reading for anyone who wants to really study their own disciplinary culture.

The CID's work implies a broad definition of the word 'discipline'. There are purists who argue that neuroscience, for example, cannot be a discipline; it is a field of study. For these people a discipline is more akin to an approach to thought. Whilst acknowledging this, for the purpose of this book, I will accept a broader definition of the word discipline. I am accepting that 'discipline' is a field of study that has its own sets of problems and questions, knowledge bases and approaches to enquiry.

Even within disciplines, academics will often be expected to take a position and from that position will privilege certain types of knowledge, for example a philosopher might take an ontological position from an existentialist or phenomenological point of view and a scientist might be positivist or relativist.

Throughout the disciplines there are similarities in the methods used to encourage enculturation, for example, doctoral students giving seminars or papers to each other and to members of the department, inviting and organising external speakers to give seminars and attending conferences is common practice. There are differences in whether students are encouraged to co-write with academics or to submit journal articles on their own, but both practices are important in enculturation. Potter argues that disciplinary communities need to be encouraged to aid critical reflection – whilst acknowledging that there are generic principles in the scholarship of teaching and learning (Potter in Murray 2008).

There are several issues that need to be disentangled here when we examine why enculturation in the disciplines is important, but not necessarily sufficient. Firstly there is a case for members of a disciplinary community being able to offer learned critique of each others work; secondly there is a case for the translation of generic teaching and learning practices into different disciplinary languages and habits (e.g. enquiry-based learning is a generic practice but it might be called a project, an investigation or an action learning set in different departments) and thirdly there is a case for good practices in one discipline to be examined for their appropriateness or helpfulness if other disciplines were to emulate them. It is to be able to explore this latter case that I now summarise aspects of the CID project in seven different disciplines (Golde & Walker 2006).

Sciences

Doctoral students working in the sciences are not usually as lonely as some in the humanities or social sciences can be. Scientists usually work long hours in laboratory teams. The doctoral student may learn as much from a neighbouring post-doctoral student as from their supervisor.

The CID project recommended that the contradictions and inconsistencies of science must be cherished; scientists must be able to take risks but also be rigorous in their work and conscious of the public context. The single most important issue is choosing and defining a problem and locating it in a larger map of the field, and this needs reassessing every two years. The approximate degree of intellectual security must be articulated. 'On-going critical reflection in the form of a departmental seminar on the state of knowledge in the discipline must be an integral part of doctoral training' (Elkana 2006: 72). A critical study of selected biographies of past caretakers of the profession should be pursued. Scientific knowledge is not always cumulative, when what has gone before is disproved; it is frequently omitted from future teaching (unless it forms a lesson in how not to do something).

Mathematics

Mathematics is an international discipline, its language is readily understood by all mathematicians, but in the past mathematicians have often divided themselves into two groups: pure and applied. They also frequently work on their own.

Algebra, number theory, probability, analysis, logic, differential equations, geometry and topology form part of pure maths which is akin to an art. Applied maths is pure maths applied to problems. Some mathematicians argue that this barrier is artificial and should be dropped. There is concern about the decline in interest in maths from Western students and two suggestions for overcoming this were: firstly to encourage team rather than the individual working which has become a norm, and secondly to encourage ownership of problems by the students creating them rather than supervisors allocating the next problem in their research programme to the next doctoral student. If pure and applied maths are to merge, the requirement for mathematicians to be able to work with multi-disciplinary teams will increase.

Mathematical knowledge tends to be cumulative, unlike sciences; new maths builds on but does not discard what has come before.

Chemistry

Doctoral students may join a lab and work for some months before they are allocated a supervisor. There are many 'grand challenges' which need the chemists' skills (e.g. develop unlimited and inexpensive energy, with new ways of energy generation, storage and transportation), but there can be problems of over-specialisation and the atomistic nature of the subject can limit doctoral students' awareness of interdisciplinary matters. The two basic aspects of a chemist's work are substances and transformation but the grand challenges mean that interdisciplinary research is vital. Chemists too must now be ready to work in multi-disciplinary teams

A useful suggestion from this discipline is that doctoral students can be usefully charged with the responsibility of inviting outside specialists for departmental colloquia.

Compared with many other fields, chemistry has far to go in achieving gender, age and racial diversity, the typical doctoral student is a 28-year-old white male. The career expectation is of a life working at the bench, yet in practice this does not always happen, and, if chemistry is to remain a central discipline, it is necessary to prepare chemists for a life where they will also need more generic skills.

Neuroscience

This is the study of the brain and brain function, and is an example of a relatively new field that embraces pharmacology, psychology, biology, biomedical sciences, nanotechnology, bioengineering, mathematics, chemistry, computing and even some sociology. Neuroscience doctoral students, therefore, will come from one disciplinary background, and will have to understand others before they can pursue their research. The challenge for neuroscience then, is to manage boundaries productively whilst retaining its core expertise. This conflict between breadth and depth can be solved to some extent by generalised training programmes to extend students' existing knowledge and laboratory rotations. The challenge is to maintain quality within this explosion of knowledge. Other disciplines define their unit of analysis automatically (e.g. molecular biology, cell biology) – the challenge for neuroscience is to bring together a top-down and a bottom-up approach in a rigorous manner. A neuroscientist needs to be aware of the trajectory of work in all adjacent disciplines; Hymen calls this a 'Janus-like' quality. One test of competence in the discipline is a pragmatic one: can a doctoral student read and criticise any paper in the field's general journals?

The journal club has been identified as a signature pedagogy for neuroscience and is customary in most biological science departments. A single article is usually presented by a member of the department; participation including doctoral students, postdoctoral researchers and academic faculty is expected. Journal clubs teach critical analysis, presenting skills and (because they are often interdepartmental) encourage interdisciplinarity. This practice effectively consolidates knowledge in a fast-moving field. Many humanities and education journals publish four or six editions a year, yet one immunology journal publishes 52 editions a year.

Education

If neuroscience is an example of how disciplinary boundaries are falling, education is an example of how one discipline can permeate every other one. Every discipline is concerned about how it is taught, so disciplinary pedagogy is of interest to all. Education also requires an ability to understand politics, psychology, sociology, philosophy, learning theories, administration, management and economics. This broad base has led critics to perceive a lack of quality in educational research but leads us to understand that doctoral students in education need not only to ensure scholarly rigour, they also need to be able to defend their paradigm to all-comers.

Everyone in the academic world has been a student at some point. Many Ed D students have also been teachers and doctoral students are likely to be mature entrants who begin their studies with strong beliefs about the nature of teaching and learning. This provides fertile soil for reflection which should extend every student's methodological understanding. Proof in education is a very elusive characteristic; it is not much of an experimental science (although there is a significant role for pilot studies) yet educationalists need to be able to speak persuasively of qualitative matters to quantitative scientists.

History

Historians can be either social science or humanities based. The notion of cultural capital is an example of a topic which moves across boundaries. History has moved to take into account different perspectives (e.g. from a western perspective to a global one); historians are creating a well-grounded narrative, but, like scientists, they have to recognise that new discoveries may make their 'knowledge' instantly redundant. These narratives are based on primary sources – documents are a vital tool of the trade. The regular seminar is a major method of teaching, when arguments will be presented in front of other students, tested and challenged.

Skills of classifying, decoding, comparing, contextualising and communicating explain why many historians undertake careers outside academia. They have to anyway, because these days there are far fewer posts for them.

English

There is a basic division in the subject between literature and composition. In English there is a recognised (if disputed) canon. This canon can be broken down into a List. The List is a group of works that forms the basis of study for a particular programme and it might comprise 60 or 100 works. At a doctoral level the student and supervisor might work together to create an acceptable list which will reflect the student's position (e.g. Romanticism or Feminism in a certain period). Mastering this list can take many solitary months.

There are some fundamental questions in English: what is national literature; what counts as the best writing; are there better or worse ways of reading texts; what is the relationship between literature and its media? There has long been a tradition of understanding that teaching a subject encourages mastery of it, and this opportunity occurs frequently for English doctoral students in the USA.

The CID project detected strong gender issues in the study of English. They argued that in the USA the subject is becoming feminised with increasing numbers of female undergraduate students, but that there is still a legacy of patronising paternalism in the hierarchy. Whilst that paternalism may or may not be gender biased, they quote a fascinating unsent letter from an English student to her professor:

> 'Too bad' she says 'I am leaving this course feeling just as separate from, intimidated by, in awe of, and ultimately uninterested in (the great texts we were being introduced to) as I was when I entered. Sometimes I wonder if that's what you actually want – to keep us from joining some charmed inner circle of knowledge.'
>
> (Abernethy 2006: 358)

Joining this charmed inner circle of knowledge is exactly what we *are* aiming to do when we use a 'communities of practice' approach to creating stewards of the discipline.

From this brief summary of some of the characteristics or ambitions of the doctoral process in different disciplines, we can see some interesting ideas emerging which could be used by other disciplines or which could become more applicable as disciplinary boundaries fade. Box 4.1 lists ten different ways that the academic could encourage the student to become a member of the discipline. The existence of this table (and those in subsequent chapters) is ironic because I am taking a functional approach to describing a range of very different approaches to research supervision.

Nurturing the intellectual community

Collegiality needs space. Universities and departments vary enormously in the space that they can create for staff and doctoral students to take breaks. In Sweden it is a social institution to have *fika*. This is a regular morning break where coffee and tea, a light snack and conversation with colleagues are shared.

Some colleges or universities aspire to grand common rooms where all the latest papers and journals are available on coffee tables surrounded by comfortable chairs. Others have less inviting environs. Some time and attention given to this can be repaid by loyalty over many years.

Box 4.1 Ten different ways to help students to be socialised into the discipline

1   Encourage the student to read the biographies of significant academics in your discipline.
2   Encourage or establish teams for students who normally work solo.
3   Encourage students who work on theoretical codes to work with teams on applications.
4   Give responsibility to doctoral students to invite quest speakers and organise colloquia.
5   Create 'the List' of essential works to be mastered (possibly an exercise for a whole course team).
6   Encourage teaching undergraduates or masters students as a form of studying.
7   Arrange for students to present arguments/papers to colleagues in your own discipline.
8   Arrange for students to present papers to colleagues from another discipline.
9   Use the seminar to encourage group learning and team building.
10   Establish journal clubs to encourage sharing, develop critical analysis and consolidate new knowledge.

Traditions can be created remarkably quickly, and including doctoral students in these events can make a great difference to a student's sense of belonging and their willingness to contribute to the life of the department.

Collegiality also needs stimulation and this can be achieved in many ways. Some examples include: bringing in experts in the discipline from other universities for scholarly seminars, making the most of visiting academics, introducing job applicants informally to the team during the interview process and introducing external examiners to colleagues.

Enculturation for international students

The framework as a whole has a western derivation but the learning archetypes it describes can be interpreted for all students regardless of where they study. 'Culture' can be defined in many ways, but for our purposes I am defining it in its anthropological sense: referring to customs, kinship, language, social practices and world view. So 'enculturation' means moving towards firstly an understanding of and then secondly a sense of belonging in a new culture. Students moving to a new country to take their postgraduate studies can acquire cultural capital, in addition to the intellectual capital which is gained through participating in the academic community. ('Capital' as Bourdieu saw it, was any resource effective in a given social area that enables someone to appropriate specific profits arising out of participation in that arena. He related the opportunity to acquire forms of capital to social class. Bourdieu 1986, 1998.) Intercultural experience supports students facing a complex and globalised world. Domestic students (and academics) also gain immeasurably from this mix of an academic qualification and cross-cultural understanding. Recent figures show that over 3 million students internationally are enrolled outside their country of citizenship, and this figure has increased rapidly from under 2 million in 2000 (OECD, 2009: 334). The Bologna Declaration (1999) aimed to create a European higher education area by 2010 where there would be a compatible degree structure to enhance student mobility between 46 countries. It aims to align quality assurance systems, a credit transfer system and create a common way of describing qualifications. In the UK in 2004 the number of overseas postgraduates as a percentage of the student body was 6.2 per cent overall, yet at the LSE this percentage was 42.2 per cent, at Cranfield it was 31.9 per cent, at UMIST it was 18.3 per cent and at Oxford, Cambridge and Imperial it was around 15 per cent (HEPI 2004). In the UK, academic institutions are also leading the way with the numbers of international students that they recruit.

In most cases this means that universities also depend on international students for a significant proportion of their fees revenue, and there are those who suggest this makes UK universities unnecessarily vulnerable. However the progress of knowledge requires us to work together globally, and the alternative is the argument of minimalisation and protectionism.

Every country needs international students, and if we are aiming to educate a globally competent postgraduate, our international students are an essential resource. It is not uncommon to have an academic from one country, supervising a student from a second country, both working in a third country and neither speaking nor writing their native language. Students are increasingly looking for the best universities in the world, not just in their country, and the measurements used by the *Times Higher Education Supplement* for the World University Rankings are informative and will become pressures in their own right. Their criteria include: academic and employer views, staff/student ratios, citations, and *numbers of international staff and students* (my emphasis) (THES 2009). The message is clear: your university will climb the international league tables by taking on more international staff and students, and we know that international students are likely to have gone through very stringent selection processes, and can be among 'the best that their country has to offer' (Krause 2007: 59).

Studies of international students find that they are used to very different learning environments – some have never experienced seminars and tutorials, others do not understand what is required of an 'essay', and some are used to studying and deeply memorising texts rather than group discussion. (Biggs

& Tang 2007, Kember 2000, Okorocha 2007). As Wisker (2005: 203) has pointed out, international students may not have done research before within a western university paradigm, so it can be useful to audit both their research and computing skills and provide early support as appropriate. An attitude of mutual research is developing strong intercultural partnerships by the Centre of Applied Linguistics at Warwick and these principles can be applied to identifying how to help our research students:

> To achieve a greater ability to understand our international partners, we require a range of qualities. We need to be open to new ideas and ready to challenge our assumptions, and we need to avoid jumping to quick opinions about the behaviour we encounter (new thinking). In terms of our own behaviour, we need to be interested in how others' goals for the project may be different from our own, and thus seek to explore and take them into account (goal orientation). In specific national cultural contexts, we also need to be pro-active in researching the national sectorial contexts, values and behaviours of the people we encounter (information gathering). In multicultural groups we need to share and surface the different perspectives people have about an issue in order to promote problem-solving and creativity (synergistic solutions).
>
> (Spencer Oatey & Stadler 2009: 2)

It is easy to make assumptions about international students and to alienate them through pedagogical practices they may be unfamiliar with. For example, how does the academic overcome the problem of the student who expects to 'receive instructions' and who believes that to do anything other than nod and agree with the teacher is poor behaviour?

Another difficult problem can be to learn the skill of critical thinking, to be able to formulate an argument, anticipate complex problems and put it coherently on paper. It is interesting that one student found it very helpful when her supervisor taught her to make arguments one paragraph at a time (Nagata in Ryan & Zuber-Skerritt 1999).

So how might international students respond to the challenge of becoming a research student in a foreign country? Wisker *et al.* (2003b) suggest that they can resort to learning behaviours that have been 'safe' in the past and overcautious contextualisation because they find it difficult to engage fully with problem solving, reflection and deep study.

It is no longer adequate to send international students to a language centre for a few hours remedial tuition. The process of enculturation takes years, one-to-one contact, open minds and hearts – research supervision can provide the ideal environment in which this can happen. International students can rightly complain if they are forced to study their topics from just one perspective, and this need to learn about different perspectives can inform and broaden supervision as well. In the UK, if the student is looking at motivation, as well as studying some traditional western theorists there may be a need to bring in other advisers, for example, on Confucian understandings or on what the Islamic 'Koran' or the Buddhist 'Tipitaka' has to say about the topic.

Academics recognise that working with international students requires different skills and is not always straightforward.

> (Some) international students ... believe that someone who is in charge of them is always right, and that everything that is published is correct. They are frightened to criticise. (... Some) have the same problems but worse because they cannot admit to failure. I would ask how an experiment went and they would say 'fine'. Yet a few weeks later problems would become obvious. I asked: 'Did you do Step 1, Step 2, and were you careful with Step 3?' They would say: 'yes'. Well obviously something had gone wrong. (Hard pure)

This sounds like more than a language problem, and needs a full diagnosis. It may need to be tackled in four stages. Firstly the language problem needs to be assessed, secondly the academic needs to ask open questions (questions which do not allow a single word answer of 'yes' or 'no'), thirdly the student needs to feel safe enough to be able to admit incomprehension, and fourthly the student may need someone to guide him/her through the experimental procedure to see if that is where the problem lies. This can be where the team approach becomes important, a post-doctoral student, another doctoral student or a sympathetic member of staff or laboratory assistant can be called in to help. Gaining cultural capital is valuable for all parties, but it requires effort and one research supervisor said:

> International students are an awful lot harder to train. You don't know that they don't know an awful lot of stuff that you would normally take for granted. I do have to send them off on modules. These people (have different experiences we need to understand and build on). (Hard pure)

All of these tasks take time and empathy, but the team approach can mean that they do not need to take quite as much time as at first appears.

Some academics feel that the carrot and stick approach is necessary; this academic was honest about his/her failings as well as those of the student:

> For some (international students coming to this country) is a real shock, they can have been quite senior in their job and used to getting other people to do things for them. What do you do to help them? You put in more time and hope to get them through. How do you get over dependency? I don't think I do. (Hard pure)

Many international postgraduates were holding down senior posts before they came abroad to study. Some of them find enormous differences in the way that student behaviour is managed, the way that authority figures are regarded and in the amount of freedom that they have. The bundle of problems that the academic above is describing needs a detailed diagnosis. Does the student understand the procedures and benchmarks (functional), feel that they belong to a team, department or cohort (enculturation), understand the western tradition of criticality and argument analysis (critical thinking) and have a desire for autonomy (emancipation)?

One of those problems was illustrated when a male PhD student said to me (a female):

> You don't realise how difficult it is for me to look you in the eye. I have been taught not to do that. (Engineering student)

Etiquette about body language, gestures and timekeeping varies significantly in different countries; innocent actions can cause offence.

Supervisors are clear that they need to understand why students are undertaking any particular programme of study. The following quotation arose in the context of a discussion about international students, but is actually true for all students:

> An awful lot of overseas students have got to have the PhD for a purpose. All the people who are coming in now are not like me. The subject is a means to an end. (Hard applied)

International students raise the same sorts of problems that national students raise.

> Cultural issues can cause problems. For example a student who got their MSc in the States expected their supervisor to do the same for them as (they had experienced) in the US. Some students think 'I have paid my fees and I expect a service'. But I think a supervisor is not a service provider. (Hard applied)

The quotations below illustrate a bundle of issues which are intertwined, they were raised in the context of discussion about international students in the interviews, but many of them could apply to home students as well. The point of quoting them here is so the reader can interrogate their own perspective. The issues raised in the quotations include:

1 Status
2 Finance
3 Attitudes to authority, dependency and failure

4 Language
5 Pressure to recruit
6 Managing current experience in the light of previous experiences.

> Some cultures will see everything in terms of relations rather than knowledge objects. You need to understand their reluctance to criticise you, which is not helpful in developing a PhD. The co-explorer dimension is not there. They are looking at things differently. (Soft pure)

The following quotation illustrates a potentially dangerous conflation of intelligence and cultural issues.

> I have a student (nearing completion) who still comes to me and asks 'what do I do next?' Maybe she is not quite as bright as she needs to be as well as any cultural/country issues, but she may have problems with the defence of her thesis. Although I will try to train her to help her to answer awkward questions. (Soft applied)

Again, another quotation that in context conflated two quite separate issues:

> Money – sometimes they end up working too much in Tesco's and this becomes a problem. (Soft applied)

> I had a student who disappeared for 3 weeks. He could not solve a problem with software and was ashamed to admit it. I try to get through to them early on 'don't do that'. (Soft pure)

Many of these quotations raise issues that are not purely cross-cultural, but they do require tactful debate to uncover stereotypes that may be held. The reward is a profound understanding.

In a focus group, international students discussed supervision and said what they most wanted. I have related some of their statements to the different approaches and this demonstrates the interrelationships between enculturation of international students and their needs across the whole framework. This does not mean that the supervisor needs to stay with any particular approach, but there may need to be a discussion about why another approach is more beneficial.

There was a strong request for **functional** support as a basis for moving forward. This student wanted to understand the stages, the structure, the numbers and frequency of meetings that can be expected:

> (We want) guidance about the process because I don't think when we all came we were aware of how the process works and the research methods

classes (did not start until later). It would be helpful if the supervisors sat down and explained the whole process and how it works ... Giving guidance throughout the project is important but particularly at the beginning ... because when they say 'read the literature', you might not know how to go about it ... About the regular meetings. I think these are important because at least you keep track of where you are and you don't take time to do things which should not take that long. (Student 4, Business studies)

The next quote acknowledges the importance of the **relationship** for an international student:

I remember when I had my first meeting with my two supervisors I was very happy and sent an e-mail back to my friend at home I told them that I sat down with my supervisors and we talk and had a nice chat and whatever and maybe we didn't have a chance before and this was important to me. (Student 8, Science)

Here there is recognition that **enculturation** was enabling the student to have a feeling of belonging:

It was very important to me, communicating and a feeling that I'm starting to participate in that kind of scientific chat, if you see. (Student 8, Science)

The importance of supporting the student by giving high-quality feedback to enable them to constructively develop their **critical thinking** skills was also emphasised:

I think I want them just to be honest about, how the work progress and be co-operative. (Student 4, Business studies)

Another student asked for recognition that research is also a personal journey and for **emancipatory** support:

My research is a bit different from the others so when we have a weekly subject group meeting and have a discussion about research, I feel I'm different from everyone else and I started to get worried about that. I went to my supervisor and told him: 'I'm feeling different and I can't understand why'. So my supervisor helped me and that was important. (Student 8, Science)

The **relationship** element came through strongly from some students:

I wanted encouragement because I'd heard so many bad stories about supervisors, telling students, 'Well you are going to fail, you're not going to pass'. I don't think this is good. (Student 5, Music)

And students need confidence in their supervisor's abilities, in this next case they want to know that the supervisor's **critical judgement** is good enough and their communication skills are clear enough to ensure that the student understands accurately where they stand:

I met an external supervisor coming for a viva and he just said that the paper was awful. I do not understand how the supervisors of that person had ... let him go on. (Student 4, Business studies)

Students want a **functionally** competent supervisor, but probably more important is to have some mutually acceptable expectations:

And please don't delay the feedback because I heard some bad stories about some people submitting a first draft of a paper and the supervisor is very busy and he or she takes two months to make the comments. I've heard bad stories. (Student 5, Music)

They also appreciate someone who can advise on opportunities for **enculturation**:

Mine's already given my advice on it, telling me which conferences to go to, to meet the right people, telling me I can get to know people and about meeting different lecturers and stuff. She's quite good like that. (Student 6, Psychology)

My supervisor has also helped me do some networking with, to start with my data collection and the hotel company that I will be working for. So he introduced the contact. He also introduced another contact ... he was very helpful. (Student 4, Business studies)

Particularly at the beginning of a relationship it is important to be clear about what standards of work are acceptable, this is a mixture of developing **critical thinking** and **enculturation** and the effect of our efforts can be unanticipated:

The first time when I wrote something ... she gave me a very detailed criticism about my work, mainly about my writing style. She gave me two examples of this: one the same way I'm writing ... and ... one I should aspire (to) ... But even so, I remember for two days I was very depressed, even though she gave me examples. And she said 'you should try', that was good, but still, it was shocking for me. For me, for my second report when I improved my work and my writing style changed and she wrote, 'that's good, and that's the way you should continue', that was encouraging. (Student 8, Science)

We could summarise from these extracts the main needs that these international students had by completing the boxes of the framework. Their needs are no different to the needs of every student. There is a conflict inherent in these expectations, of course – some students want more guidance than the academic believes they should be giving, some students want more hand-holding over living arrangements than the academic believes is their responsibility and some students want honest feedback, but not too critical because it might just be too harsh. Making these judgements is the joy of supervision – seeing a student motivated and eager to get on with their work is exciting. If we meet often enough, generally even if we get it wrong in one supervisory meeting, we can learn from that and rectify it later. Box 4.2 lists some questions that the academic can use to assess the skills and knowledge that they have and those they might need to acquire to be able to successfully work with all students.

Creating a mutually supportive cohort of students

Most research students will have some taught sessions on research methods. Some strategic learners resent learning more than the minimum that they need for their particular project, but students with a deeper approach recognise that the more knowledge and skills they acquire now, the better their careers may be served in future (Entwistle 2007, Prosser & Trigwell 1999).

An early example of an innovative taught programme was designed by Elton and Pope (1989) when they used a term of regular weekly sessions for both staff and students to lead a variety of seminars. They argued that this approach overcame some of the isolation experienced by students in social sciences and humanities. Journal clubs can fulfil the same function in science-based groups. Well-designed research methods training programmes also provide students with an opportunity to meet other staff experts as well as other students.

Although enculturation and emancipation appear to be opposites, there are a couple of quotations below which show how difficult it can be to distinguish between them. In the end I would argue that this first quote is an example of enculturation – the student is being given differing opinions about which is the best type of academic paper, but the message is still that writing good academic papers (and by implication, the academic life) is something to be aspired to.

Box 4.2 Self assessment questions to test skills and knowledge about working with international students

Recruitment

1   Are you taking enough care over recruitment, especially over doctoral research students? Do you interview them by phone or in person, do you ask for examples of written work and written confirmation of funding arrangements for the whole period of study before accepting them as students?

Induction

2   Do you arrange an additional induction programme for international students so that they know who to go to for support and advice on linguistic, personal, financial, religious and family matters?
3   Do you arrange a special time to discuss methods of learning and teaching used on your programmes? Do you discuss what you mean by 'supervision', 'referencing' and what you mean by 'independent work and research'? Do you give all students examples of the standard of work you are looking for? Do you audit students' research and computing skills to assess what support they need?
4   Have you established a good relationship with key staff in your language centre/international office/library/student counselling centre, so you can refer students to them and fully understand yourself what support is available for your students?

Giving feedback

5   Can you give all students verbal and written guidance on the processes they need to engage with in order to successfully pass your programme?
6   Do you encourage your students early in the programme to start writing. Do you timetable opportunities for you to give them clear feedback so that they can develop their writing skills, and have time to improve?
7   Being sensitive to differences
8   Do you explain etiquette in your country and institution's education system? Do you sensitively offer to exchange information about timekeeping, gender relationships and body language?
9   Are you aware of the etiquette in other cultures; are you aware of major religious festivals and national requirements for your students?
10 Do you know what food and drink is acceptable to most world religions?

I like big chunky papers that really are very scholarly and comprehensive in their approach. I have a colleague, a very close colleague, my closest colleague who has a completely different view. His view is a paper should contain no more than one idea and that's what he tries to publish and we totally disagree on it ... And I tell students we have different views on this, this is what I believe, this is what I grew up on, here is the evidence where I think it is important but other people look at it differently and they can try for themselves but at least expose them to the issue and the debate. (Soft applied)

This second quotation is similarly an example of enculturation, even though it is about encouraging students to help each other. It is a good example of an academic creating a cohort of mutually supportive students.

They need people to discuss ideas and issues with, you know ... models, read their paper, give them detailed comments etc. So I found that the number of students I had started to get to be fairly large and what I decided to do was to try and take advantage of the fact that they are all (there and get them) to help each other, I organised a, kind of, a weekly lunch where we all eat over lunch and had someone responsible for making a presentation. (Soft applied)

Enculturation is an important part of supervision, especially early on. It means a good induction process, welcoming and helping students to become a member of the discipline and helping them to feel at home in the department. It is a powerful concept in developing academics, it is one that needs to be used with care lest students perceive it as coercive, but open discussions about what students hope to do in the next stage of their lives will help the academic to know how to handle this. If the student eventually decides that they do want to follow a different career path, the academic can step back, content in the knowledge that their student is making an informed decision.

In this chapter we have explored the power of enculturation in enabling students who research to create an identity for themselves and develop a sense of belonging. This supports setting standards of acceptable work, but also needs to be critically examined to ensure it is not stifling. The voice of some of the international students reminds us that they have needs which supervisors can meet by employing a range of approaches. In the next chapter we look at critical thinking within the disciplines and explore epistemological and metacognitive development.

Further reading

Global People. http://www.globalpeople.org.uk Publications from a project on intercultural awareness from the Centre for Applied Linguistics at the University of Warwick that were funded by HEFCE are available for download from this website.

Grant, B. M. (2008) 'Agonistic struggle: Master–slave dialogues in humanities supervision'. *Arts and Humanities in Higher Education.* 7.1: 9–27.

Lave, J. and Wenger, E. (1991) *Situated Learning: Legitimate Peripheral Participation.* Cambridge: Cambridge University Press.

Neumann, R. (2001) 'Disciplinary differences and university teaching'. *Studies in Higher Education* 26.2: 135–146.

Shacham, M. and Od Cohen, Y. (2009) 'Rethinking PhD learning incorporating communities of practice'. *Innovations in Education and Teaching International.* 46.2: 279–292.

Chapter 5

Developing critical thinking

The critical thinking approach: an introduction

This approach has four aspects to it: firstly an understanding of different beliefs about knowledge and an ability to assess statements in relation to those beliefs, secondly an ability to define and evaluate the argument in a manner appropriate to the relevant discipline or discipline(s), thirdly an ability to solve problems in a logical manner and finally to be able to reflect metacognitively on performance.

The term 'critical thinking' is used here to describe the intellectual, philosophical and analytical approaches to problem solving that the academic will need to enable the student to use. It is about developing in the student an ability to understand, critique and create the argument. It is an approach in which we deliberately depersonalise the relationship and the student, so that we can examine the substantive thinking processes free from emotion. In practice, of course, we cannot depersonalise the student – the relationship is hugely important; however it is important to establish what the goals might be before feelings have to be taken into account.

At the early stages of outlining a thesis Murray (2006) suggests a (relatively) simple exercise that the researcher supervisor can encourage a student to undertake. She suggests that students use between 25 and 50 words to complete each of the following sentences:

1 My research question is …
2 Researchers who have looked at this subject are …
3 They argue that …
4 A argues that …
5 B argues that …
6 Debate centres on …
7 There is still work to be done on …
8 My research is closest to that of …
9 My contribution will be …
     (Adapted from Murray 2006)

There have been many attempts to identify the different thinking styles used by different disciplines, and we will explore some of these. However, disciplines are on the move, and it is no longer sufficient for a student to be master of one disciplinary approach to thinking. Golde and Walker (2006) describe how students entering doctoral studies in neuroscience can have come from backgrounds in biology, psychology, chemistry or pharmacology (p. 207) and even sociologists are bringing insights to bear on the problems that neuroscientists are involved in. Environmental science is another example of a 'hybrid discipline'; it requires engineering, chemistry, management and psychological understanding. Some music technology courses now demand a high level of competence in physics and computer science, and these are considered as important as any musical background.

One academic was quite clear what they were looking for:

> An excellent thesis is written in a crystal clear fashion. Well structured. Appropriate style of language, not excessively technical. One which at every point explains and justifies what they have done. A weak thesis describes procedure but does not justify it. (Hard pure)

An alternative view was put forward by this academic

> What do I expect them to learn – it depends of course a little bit on their future career plans. But … I expect them to learn how to learn, that's one thing, I expect them to learn how to reason, I expect them learn how to start into something totally new. I mean one of the things you learn on a PhD is to think of a new experiment, to design a new experiment and carry it out and then defend your result by publication and talks to your colleagues, and those are skills you can use in many disciplines, in many different environments … from academia to industry to government jobs or venture capitalist, to finance, you name it. So I really want them to have an independence, an ability to step into the unknown and make a contribution to knowledge and society. (Hard pure)

And a third view encouraging questioning the nature of reality:

> They need to know what is mind dependent and what is mind independent. How do you know something is independent? Like what we are doing now (the interview), is it social constructivism in action because it is relying upon memory rather than a transcendental phenomenological position? (Soft pure)

The purpose of this chapter is to try to look at critical thinking from both a disciplinary and a more philosophical point of view. A synthesis of the ideas that emerge from this investigation is then used to inform the types of critical thinking questions that the academic might want to encourage the research student to ponder.

Research is, by its nature, at the boundary of known knowledge, and academics may be confronted by students who want or need to take an interdisciplinary approach to their studies. This often leads to the recruitment of co-academics, but it also requires the academic to have an understanding of the ways of thinking that lie behind different disciplines.

Traditionally, critical thinking is considered to be at the heart of the PhD supervision. Browne and Freeman (2000) offer the following definition: 'critical thinking comes in many forms, but all possess a single core feature. They presume that human arguments require evaluation if they are to be worthy of widespread respect. Hence critical thinking focuses on a set of skills and attitudes that enable a listener or reader to apply rational criteria to the reasoning of speakers and writers' (p. 301).

Stevenson and Brand (2006) point out that critical thinking is largely a western, secularist intellectual tradition, and we need to be sensitive to this when applying it in different cultures or to some disciplines. Critical thinking is a western philosophical tradition that encourages analysis, looking for propositions and arguments for and against them. The roots of this approach to supervision are both dialectic and dialogic.

There can be barriers to developing critical thinking through writing:

> A student might implement corrections and think that is good enough to pass. They think 'this has been through the filter of the supervisor, therefore it is OK'. (Soft pure)

Critical thinking is not developed in the same way in every culture. In Confucian societies:

> the role of the scholar was to discover those rules set down in these texts, requiring an intensive study of the limited texts within the reference. Study was often rendered as commentary and exegesis rather than a synthesis of different views presented in the form of an individual argument. The role of reading was to (re)discover what the sage was saying.
>
> (Smith 1999: 149)

In practice it addresses such questions as what is the underlying conceptual framework, what are the arguments for and against, what has been considered and what has been left out. Wisker (2005) argues that practising using the metalanguage of viva defence is a very useful supervisory skill because it ensures that the student addresses gaps in knowledge, boundaries and methodology.

Critical thinking implies a 'researcher absent' process (Brew 2001, Pearson & Brew 2002) and is only part of the model suggested by Barnett (1997) of 'critical being'.

One version of this process has been called 'gentle Socratic inquiry' (Jackson 2001). The 'gentle' is inserted to counteract the image of Socratic inquiry where the consummate lawyer cleverly manipulates his adversary into a position of 'got you'. Whilst the common perception of the Socratic method is a methodical questioning and cross-examining, peeling away layers of half-truths and exposing hidden assumptions, the gentler Socratic method proposed by Jackson assumes a position of co-operative inquiry and accepts that there is no right answer.

Dialogical thinking requires examination and synthesis of a series of propositions. It includes looking at a topic from different points of view or frames of reference. When thinking dialectically, students will be testing the strengths and weaknesses of opposing points of view by putting different points of view in competition with each other. Debates and trials are two examples of dialectical thinking.

Hegel articulated the desire to look for a hidden logic, which assumes that there is one (Ravenscroft, Wegerif & Hartley, 2007). Holbrook *et al.* (2007) identified an ability to synthesise literature and make a coherent argument as a key activity evaluated by thesis examiners.

However, other writers support constructive controversy. Johnson and Johnson (2001) argue that more than 40 studies indicate that constructive inquiry produces higher achievement and retention than concurrence-seeking debate. The stages they recommend are:

1 Reaching a position on an issue
2 Being challenged and becoming uncertain about one's views (epistemic curiosity)
3 Actively searching for more information and reconceptualising one's knowledge in an attempt to resolve the uncertainty
4 Reaching a new and refined conclusion.

This approach focuses on the quality of argument, and the process can move through three stages: problematising, finding connections and uncovering conceptions/the shape of an answer.

Whether the academic is opting for being gently Socratic or constructively critical, there are various tools and questions that the academic can use to aid critical thinking; these are outlined in Table 5.1 and Box 5.1.

In the interviews with academics it became apparent that critical thinking was a discrete element of doctoral supervision. It is a strand which concentrates on the student's intellectual development. Whilst for the purposes of the analysis in this chapter we mostly ignore the psychosocial elements of supervision, in practice developing skills in critical thinking need not be a depersonalising experience.

Jones (2009) examined how critical thinking was viewed in five different disciplines: history, physics, economics, law and medicine. In interviews with

Table 5.1 Coding questions that academics might ask to develop critical thinking skills in their postgraduate students (adapted from Donald 2002: 26–27)

Thinking processes and behaviours		Typical questions the academic might ask
DESCRIPTION		Describe what you think we are looking at here.
	Identify context	What are the surroundings in which this is happening?
	State conditions	What elements of this context are essential prerequisites to this happening?
	State facts	What generally accepted information applies here?
	State functions	What normally happens here?
	State assumptions	What assumptions or propositions have been accepted? What do you mean by …?
		What is your reason for proffering that opinion? But in another situation the converse is true?
	State goal	What is your aim, what are your objectives?
SELECTION		What were the other options you looked at? Why was this chosen in preference to them?
	Choose relevant information	What information is particularly relevant to this question?
	Order information in importance	How do you prioritise it?
	Identify critical elements	What are the important units or parts of that information?
	Identify critical relations	Which connections are most important?
REPRESENTATION		What symbols are relevant here?
	Recognise organising principles	What laws or rules cover this part of the picture?
	Organise elements and relations	What does a concept map of this area look like?
	Illustrate elements and relations	What are the words or symbols that describe the links between the concepts?
	Modify elements and relations	What connections or concepts can be altered, and how?

INFERENCE		
	Discover new relations between elements	If x is true, what are the implications? What conclusions can you draw from your findings? Describe connections between concepts or elements that have not been seen before.
	Discover new relations between relations	Describe connections between these connections.
	Discover equivalence	Is that like anything else?
	Categorise	What classification does that fall into?
	Order	Where in the sequence does it fall?
	Change perspective	What if you were to look at it from another perspective?
	Hypothesise	Does this analysis help you to form a proposition?

SYNTHESIS		
	Combine parts to form a whole	Can you see a whole pattern emerging?
	Elaborate	Describe that pattern in more detail?
	Generate missing links	Where are the gaps, what does it not explain?
	Develop a course of action	How can we prove, expand, and/or illuminate this phenomena?

VERIFICATION		
		How can we test the validity of this finding? What examples can you give, what evidence can you show?
	Compare alternative outcomes	Is there any consistency across different contexts, over different times?
	Compare outcome to standard	How does this result compare to what might be expected?
	Judge validity	What is the soundness of these results? In how many ways could we prove it wrong? Would we get the same result if we used different experimental methods?
	Use feedback	What feedback are we getting? How do we need to adjust to it?
	Confirm results	What test–retest or triangulation strategies do we need to employ? Are the findings repeatable?

Box 5.1 Helping students to critically examine their work

Typical questions to ask the student:

1 Describe what you think we are looking at here. What is the context in which this is happening? What are the most important elements? What are your goals?
2 What are the key concepts here and how are they linked?
3 What are the implications of your findings? What is your proposition?
4 What patterns are emerging, describe them in more detail, and are there any gaps?
5 In how many ways could this be disproved?

---

37 academics from two Australian universities she identified that critical thinking in history related to examining evidence and context, discussing complexities and ambiguities, awareness of gaps and silences, awareness of political and ideological dimensions and the questioning of received wisdom. For physicists, she argued that critical thinking was about examining rigour, accuracy, uncertainty, predictive powers, assumptions and discussion about areas of uncertainty and the frontiers of knowledge. Economists, she said, understood critical thinking as the application of theory to practical or policy issues, whilst lawyers saw it as a process of examination of argument, evidence, logic, assumptions, social context, ethics and questioning received wisdom. For those studying medicine, she found critical thinking was about clinical reasoning, the use of evidence-based medicine, awareness of ethical issues, professional reflection and the questioning of received wisdom. The themes in this collection, whilst they have different balances in different disciplines, are similar: they are about seeing knowledge as external or constructed and contextual, as evidence based, ethically concerned and requiring rigorous investigation.

Thinking skills

Donald (2002) looked in detail at thinking in several different disciplines (physics, engineering, chemistry, biological sciences, psychology, law, education and English literature), and identified six key components of critical thinking as they applied to each discipline. Table 5.1 has an abstraction of the key components and some illustrations of lines of enquiry that academics might pursue. Donald (2002) gives many further examples for each of the disciplines she has studied.

1. Description

Description can be similar to 'defining the problem'. Establishing what is known and what is unknown is a key part of the literature survey. If a 'fact' is considered to be a generally accepted hypothesis, then describing and questioning this is part of the work to be done at this stage.

2. Selection

The literature survey and the subsequent research also require the student to select what is important. This is developing a key skill in judgement and this skill can be transferred on to many environments. One American supervisor (advisor) demonstrated the transferability of this skill when he said:

> so I'm actually not concerned about exactly what has been learned, as much as how they learn how to become scientists, how to choose what they do, to recognise what is important, how to establish their own research programmes. (Hard pure)

3. Representation

Understanding the key symbols and concepts is a vital stage in critical thinking. Mathematical and scientific symbols are one key way of doing this. Concept maps are increasingly used as a way of mapping understanding. A concept map consists of boxes which describe the key concept and linking words which describe how they are related. The links might be about causality or categorisation so they will be phrases such as *x depends upon y*, or *x is part of y*, or *x occurs when y is happening*.

Figure 5.1 is a sample concept map designed to explore effective teaching at masters level. The software used is taken from a web site established to help people draw their own maps and can be downloaded from that site: http://cmap.ihmc.us/Publications/ResearchPapers/TheoryCmaps/ TheoryUnderlyingConceptMaps.htm There is also further information on concept mapping in work by Kinchin and Hay (2007).

4. Inference

This stage of critical thinking asks the student to make a hypothesis about their findings. It expects ideas to be formulated about what might be going on, putting different analyses together to suggest links or outcomes. It is the stage at which well-formed propositions can be made.

Swartz and Perkins (1990) identify two types of inference: deductive and inductive. Deductive inference uses a logical form and includes symbolic logic. It includes propositions (and, or, not, if ... then) and quantificational

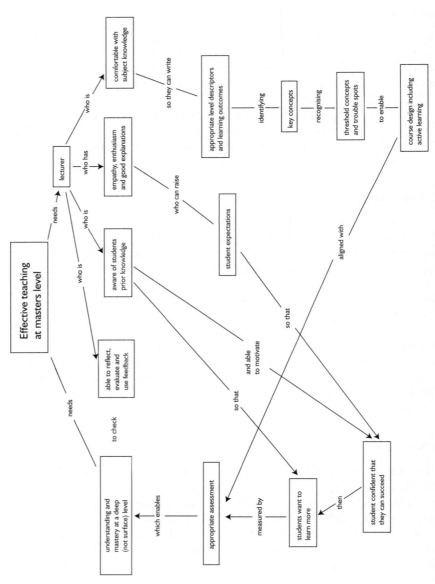

Figure 5.1 A sample concept map – effective teaching at masters level

logic. Inductive inference arises from sampling and generalisation, an analysis of cause and chance, using the scientific method, assessing probability and applying statistical techniques.

5. Synthesis

Creativity can be an important part of both inference and synthesis. It is the time when the student needs to be encouraged to stand back and look at the whole picture to see what is really emerging. A key critical skill required here is the ability to spot the gaps, either where data is missing or where the data does not fit the theory.

6. Testing validity

Another important principle is to identify what each discipline accepts as 'proof'. How does the student establish whether or not their findings are valid? Disciplines have different perspectives on this, if multi-disciplinary research is planned it is helpful to look at these individually and then decide which or which combination is appropriate.

'*Coherence*' is a word used to evaluate work in the humanities (does the explanation take account of all or most of the available facts?). In physics 'coherence' would not be used because of its association with wave theory, but physicists would be looking for *consistency*, some scientists look for internal and external consistency and see these as different phenomena. Some researchers look for consistency amongst different subject groups or situations. *Reliability over time* is another factor, and researchers may need to ask whether or not the same answer would be achieved at a different time. It is perhaps surprising that the *principle of falsification* (that a hypothesis can only be accepted if it has been subject to rigorous processes to disprove it) is not as widely used in scientific work as might be expected.

Empirical evidence supporting the proposal showing that 'it works' is considered as important by many in both humanities and the sciences. However, this *empirical justification* does not answer subsequent questions about causes, antecedents or results. *Triangulation* is a concept used in the social sciences – if we use three different research methods to look at these phenomena, do those three different methods give us the same answer?

Some of the quotations from the interviews which relate to the critical thinking approach are below and these are related to the analysis of thinking processes and behaviours described in Table 5.1. These are tentative allocations to Donald's categories for illustrative purposes, because we would need to understand more about the whole context of the research project in question to be certain about where they fitted.

They need to explain to me: 'why, what and how'. (Soft applied)

This could be an example of **description** (state facts and conditions).

> I use 'magic' words to help them identify the thread in their argument, e.g. arguably, conversely, unanimously, essentially, early on, inevitably etc. (Soft applied)

This could be an example of **inference** (discover equivalence).

> I think my student is more geared up towards reporting than thinking. I told her to shift into second gear. Her thinking is there but it does not come out in her writing. I am going to inspire her to be brave and give her some tips on how to present her data and make her voice more distinctive. I am going to encourage her to use fill-in words such as 'conversely' to synthesise and structure thoughts. (Soft applied)

This could be an example of **description** (state goal) and **inference** (change perspective).

The movement towards independence is evident once again in this category:

> I avoid dependency by getting them to think about some problems and giving them resources. (Hard applied)

This could be an example of **selection** (prioritising).

> I want them to stand on their own feet and challenge the thinking. (Hard applied)

This could be an example of **synthesis** (combining parts to form a whole).

> My tutor was not confrontational, she encouraged me to be critical of my own ideas. (Soft applied)

This could be an example of **inference** (change perspective).

> At the end of the process I want the student to have the maturity to know when a good idea is worth following or not. (Hard applied)

This could be an example of **selection** (importance).

> I will not compromise my results; they have to be 100 per cent solid. And the only way to be sure I can be 100 per cent solid about those results is to involve many people who check each others' work and who have the same high standards. (Hard pure)

This could be an example of **verification**.

> I would say the data is king, I mean they have to follow what the data is telling them. (They must) not let the data be obscured, (they must) be completely honest about it, (they must) not to be afraid to say: 'look I don't understand it. It's not telling what I think it is. It's telling me something different'. (Hard pure)

This could be an example of **representation, inference and verification**.

> To me the best students are the ones who are the most independent, the most able to identify ... they have a sense of identifying what they want to do, why they want to do things, they are always asking those kind of questions, why am I doing what I'm doing?, why is it important? How can I do the most important thing possible? (Hard pure)

This could be an example of **selection and inference**.

Table 5.1 was quite detailed; Box 5.1 gives a shorter list which might be useful in some cases.

How does knowledge appear?

There is another basic question to be considered in relation to critical thinking – are there any differences in how knowledge emerges or appears in different disciplines? Table 5.1 suggests so many overlaps across the disciplines that there is no particular disciplinary pattern. Mathematics was not one of the disciplines studied by Donald and some argue that mathematicians understand knowledge differently because they are working within man-made rules and patterns. Once a mathematical formula is proven, unlike a scientific, artistic or social scientific one, it is not going to be disproven. Some mathematicians argue that at its peak or its edge, their subject becomes an art form and therefore can also be subjectively appreciated. Many students struggle with the notion of conditional and provisional thinking, however at doctoral level one supervisor observed:

> Most students do make the leap from dogmatic to provisional thinking. (Soft pure)

Beliefs about knowledge are an important part of understanding critical thinking. Knowledge can be examined in several ways. These include looking at it as a socially constructed process and/or as an inductive/deductive process (Biggs & Tang 2007). Propositional and practical knowledge are more recognisable within traditional forms of education, and they can be integrated with two other forms of knowledge, experiential and imaginal

(Gregory 2006b) or divided into hard/soft/pure and applied, as Biglan (1973a, 1973b) originally did.

The transcripts of interviews with academics were analysed to see if there were different ways in which knowledge emerged. Knowledge was seen as having different properties and the sorts of comments that academics made suggested that they saw knowledge as:

- being personally experienced, risky, exciting and transforming
- useful when applied
- constrained by procedures
- controversial, contested and provisional
- emerging
- moving, growing and unbounded
- constructed through dialogue
- can be absolute and verifiable
- different in different contexts, for example in different cultures
- creative
- measured differently in arts and sciences
- hidden, tacit, not easy to classify.

These comments were turned into a poster (Figure 5.2) and academics from different disciplines were invited to show how they thought knowledge appeared in their subject. From the excited discussions around the poster, it would appear that further research would be interesting.

If we look behind the concepts that emerged from the interviews we find several key beliefs:

1 Knowledge is provisional or absolute (for example 'constructivism' supposes that we create our own knowledge and 'atomism' supposes that knowledge consists of units that are linked to each other).
2 Knowledge can be created and constructed.
3 There are procedures that constrain the emergence of knowledge.
4 Knowledge is sometimes hidden, can be risky and personally transforming.
5 Knowledge is different in different contexts and cultures.

These key beliefs are not mutually exclusive. They can be portrayed as parts of a whole as in Figure 5.3.

The academic needs to be aware that they will have views on what knowledge is, and so will their student. Perry researched the intellectual and moral growth of Harvard students. Belenky carried out a similar study from a feminist perspective and Baxter Magolda synthesised these works and carried out her own research in the United States on students in the first five years of study from undergraduate to the first year at work. These seminal

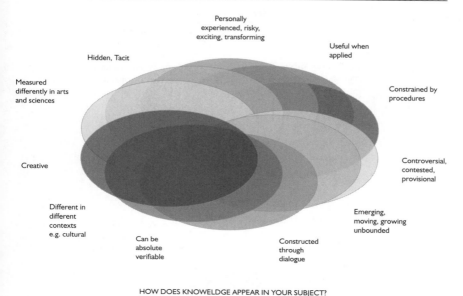

HOW DOES KNOWELDGE APPEAR IN YOUR SUBJECT?
Results of interviews with doctoral supervisors and students

Figure 5.2 Summarising quotations from academics about knowledge

works of Perry (1970), Belenky, Clinchy, Goldberger and Tarule (1986) and
Baxter Magolda (1992) can be compared in the same schema, and overall
they suggest that students move through different stages of beliefs about
knowledge. The section that follows offers one way of synthesising these
stages.

Belenky *et al.* identified 'silence' as being a first stage particularly
experienced by some women. The next stage was called 'dualism' by Perry,
and refers to a belief in absolutism and there being right or wrong answers.
Belenky *et al.* called this 'received knowing' and Baxter Magolda called this
'absolute knowing' where the academic's wisdom is received and accepted
as accurate by the student. The role of the student is to master this absolute
knowledge.

The next stage identified by Perry as 'multiplicity', by Belenky *et al.* as
'subjective knowing' and by Baxter Magolda as 'transitional knowing'
refers to a stage where it is recognised that there are a range of beliefs and
everyone's opinions are regarded as valid and valuable. Knowledge is certain
in some areas and uncertain in others.

Relativism (Perry), 'procedural knowing' (Belenky) and 'independent
knowing' (Baxter Magolda) refers to a stage of becoming aware of the need
to find and provide objective and independent evidence.

The fourth and final stage of commitment (Perry), 'constructed knowing'
(Belenky *et al.*) and 'contextual knowing (Baxter Magolda) is when individuals

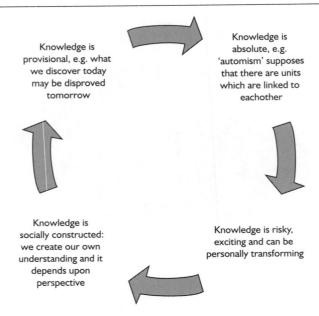

Figure 5.3 Circle of beliefs about knowledge from interviews with doctoral supervisors

recognise that knowledge depends upon its context and they decide which points of view or which analytical systems they will espouse according to the context they are in. This stage can also be described as 'self-authorship' when the individual independently makes up their own mind.

These phases arise largely out of studies of undergraduates, but there is doubt that all, or even most, undergraduates move through all the phases before they graduate. One study demonstrated that over five years, Spanish students of education developed a small but positive change in their understanding about the complexity of knowledge (epistemology), but there was little or no development in their beliefs about learning. (Rodriguez & Cano 2007). It could be argued that the fourth phase of independent self-authorship is exactly where we want our doctoral students to end up, and we would not expect them to get there until they had done a considerable amount of guided and independent study as well as a significant piece of research.

Knowing where students are in terms of their beliefs about knowledge, enables the academic to frame the next set of questions or reading. As Donald (2002) suggests, if a student understands law as paradigmatic, they are able to frame negotiations differently. For example a lawyer spends a great deal of time negotiating: is it about interpersonal relationships, social justice, justice, precedence or custom and practice?

Cox (2008) found that academics also go through different stages in terms of their beliefs about students. And we do need to ask whether we, as teachers and supervisors are somewhere between seeking to get the 'right answers' out of our students (dualism) or whether we are taking a view on different learning and teaching styles and adapting our own approach appropriately (contextual knowing). Are we in the stage of 'blaming the student' if there is poor learning or have we made a scholarly decision to investigate what is going on both in the student's cognate world and in our own?

Cox (2008) put the work of these three key theorists into a table of cognitive-structural development theories. His table can be extended to compare it with the work of King and Kitchener (Moseley *et al.* 2004). See Table 5.2.

Perry, Belenky and Baxter Magolda all used semi-structured interviews as their research method. King and Kitchener (1994) asked subjects to work with ill-structured problems and then discussed with them their experience of the process. They identified seven stages of beliefs about knowledge and reasoning and argued that while individuals pass through these stages in the order specified, they can also operate across a range of stages at any point in time.

King and Kitchener add to our understanding because they emphasise the role of developing reflective judgement. They argued that their stages 1–3 represent pre-reflective thought, stages 4 and 5 represent quasi-reflective thought and stages 6 and 7 represent reflective thought. For them reflective thought meant constructed and contextual knowing, and this is one way of looking at the level of knowing that we expect from our postgraduate students.

Barnett (2009) argues, from the point of view of a social philosopher, that propositional knowledge has been undervalued in recent times and the emphasis has swung too far towards 'becoming' through vehicles such as the skills agenda. Another perspective on knowledge, which extends these two categories of propositional knowledge and personal, ontological change, has emerged in the humanistic psychology movement. Heron (1999) has trained many facilitators and described four forms of knowing: conceptual (propositional, factual), practical (skill based), experiential and imaginal. The imaginal is explored through metaphor – it is the least understood and potentially the most powerful.

It appears that we can be at different stages in our beliefs about knowledge according to the subject, so these stages are contextual and not necessarily age dependent. Understanding the emergence of knowledge may also be related to the principles of connoisseurship which are used to analyse quality and progress in the creative arts. Box 5.2 has some questions that an academic can ask themselves to establish both their own and their students' beliefs about knowledge

Table 5.2 Cognitive-structural development theories (Cox 2008 adapted to include King and Kitchener's seven-stage model)

Perry (1970) Positions	Belenky et al. (1986) Perspectives		Baxter Magolda (1992) Stages		King and Kitchener's (1994) seven-stage model
	Silence				
Dualism	Received knowing		Absolute knowing		1. Knowing is limited to single concrete observations: what a person observes is true. Discrepancies are not noticed.
			Receiving	Mastering	2. Two categories for knowing: right answers and wrong answers. Good authorities have knowledge; bad authorities lack knowledge. Differences can be resolved by more complete information.
Multiplicity	Subjective knowing		Transitional knowing		3. In some areas, knowledge is certain and authorities have knowledge. In other areas, knowledge is temporarily uncertain; only personal beliefs can be known.
			Interpersonal	Impersonal	4. The concept that knowledge is unknown in several specific cases can lead to the abstract generalisation that knowledge is uncertain. Knowledge and justification are poorly differentiated.
Relativism	Procedural knowing		Independent knowing		5. Knowledge is uncertain and must be understood within a context; thus justification is context-specific. Knowledge is limited by the perspective of the person who knows.
	Connected	Separate	Interindividual	Individual	
Commitment	Constructed knowing		Contextual knowing		6. Knowledge is uncertain, but constructed by comparing evidence and opinion on different sides of an issue or across contexts.
					7. Knowledge is the outcome of a process of reasonable enquiry. This principle is equivalent to a general principle across domains. Knowledge is provisional.

Box 5.2 Self assessment questions to help us assess our understanding of knowledge vis-à-vis the student

1 Can you define epistemology?
2 Are we seeking to get the 'right answers' out of our students (dualism) or taking a view on different learning and teaching styles and adapting our own approach appropriately (contextual knowing)?
3 Are we at the stage of 'blaming the student' if there is poor learning or have we made a scholarly decision to investigate what is going on both in the student's cognate world and in our own?

Threshold concepts

Threshold concepts describe another way of looking at how students master knowledge, they are concepts that are critical to the understanding of the discipline and Meyer and Land (2006: 7–8) describe them as having at least the following five characteristics:

- Transformative: where the learner's view of the subject and frequently themselves is transformed
- Integrative: where they make sense of previously unrelated elements
- Irreversible: once the subject is understood through this lens, it cannot be 'unlearned'
- Bounded: the concept does not explain the whole of the discipline, but specific aspects of it
- Troublesome: it is difficult and challenging.

Most of the work on threshold concepts has been concentrated on the undergraduate curriculum, but there is evidence emerging that threshold concepts are involved in the idea of what it is to be a researcher (Kiley 2009). Examples of threshold concepts in literature which have been discussed at the doctoral level include the concept of irony, fantasy, parallels, analogies, the abstract (Wisker & Robinson 2009). There are links between threshold concepts and the work of Mezirow on transformative learning, which is introduced in the next chapter.

Problem solving

Problem solving is part of critical thinking, but it also has elements of action implied within it. It can be linked to project planning in terms of skills, and requires some critical thinking skills, planning skills and some people management skills.

Swartz and Perkins (1990) describe a typical problem-solving procedure which I have adapted here to include elements of implementation suggested by Coverdale (Taylor 1979). (See Figure 5.4.) There are three key stages: description, investigation and implementation. The descriptive stage can call upon similar critical thinking skills to those introduced by Donald above, but Swartz and Perkins add in specifically an evaluation of working in an uncertain world. This leads to the need for a risk assessment of each option eventually identified (which is part of the dialectical procedure).

This problem-solving procedure also introduces the concepts of key values. Ethical issues were discussed briefly in Chapter 3, but it is obvious that they cannot and should not be kept out of the picture when we are considering critical thinking.

The investigation stage should provide much of the information needed for the implementation stage. For example, if the necessary resources come as a surprise in the final phase, it means that the investigation was not thoroughly carried out.

For the planning and implementation stage there are a variety of project planning tools available, as we saw in Chapter 3. Figure 5.4 summarises the links between the functional and critical thinking approaches, as applied to project planning and a version of this simple staged approach can be used by students at all levels to help them design a research project.

Metacognition

Metacognition refers to observing, reflecting and directing our thinking. The question is how do we teach students to do this? The ability to reflect at a high level is not required only by those undertaking social science degrees. Academics from the hard pure subject groups spoke of the need for students to learn from mistakes and how coming to terms with failure could make them better scientists in the long run. We look at how to deal with this type of situation more in the next chapter on emancipation.

Definitions of reflection

The term 'reflective thinking' was used by John Dewey (1933) to describe the thinking process people use when faced with questions of controversy or doubt for which their current understanding or solution for whatever reason, is no longer satisfactory. According to Dewey, a 'reflective judgement' is the end goal of good thinking: the judgement or solution that brings closure to the problem (if only temporarily).

The definition of reflective learning provided by Boud, Keogh and Walker (1985: 19) states that reflection is about providing intellectual and affective activities for learners to explore their experiences 'in order to lead to new understandings and appreciations'.

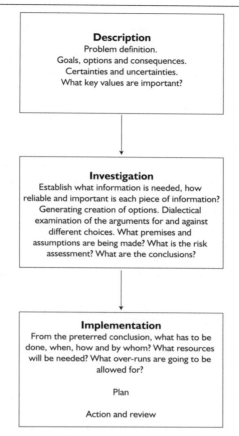

Description
Problem definition.
Goals, options and consequences.
Certainties and uncertainties.
What key values are important?

Investigation
Establish what information is needed, how
reliable and important is each piece of information?
Generating creation of options. Dialectical
examination of the arguments for and against
different choices. What premises and
assumptions are being made? What is the risk
assessment? What are the conclusions?

Implementation
From the preterred conclusion, what has to be
done, when, how and by whom? What resources
will be needed? What over-runs are going to be
allowed for?

Plan

Action and review

Figure 5.4 A problem-solving procedure

A comprehensive overview of reflection as an aid to learning was carried out by Moon (2000) which largely built upon and evaluated the work of Schon (1991) and Brookfield (1995). Schon looks at the reflective practitioner as someone who remains open to discovery and seeks that discovery by reviewing and reflecting on their actions. As Moon also points out, Schon's famous distinction between reflection-in-action and reflection-on-action may not always be clear cut and in his original work he discusses whether reflection-in-action is possible for the artist, or whether deconstruction ruins the art form.

Brookfield (1995) argues strongly for reflection when he asks teachers to 'build in some element of self-evaluation whereby students can show you that they are learning, even if to you their progress seems non-existent' (p. 180).

There is growing belief that solidifying the reflective part of Kolb's experiential learning cycle aids student learning. The original learning cycle had four separate stages which suggested that (1) learning took place when action and experimentation became (2) conscious experience which the individual used to (3) reframe their understanding of what was happening; this act of reframing led to (4) generalisation and the creation of theory (Cowan 2008).

Another dynamic model of reflection adopted is represented by the flow chart which also becomes a continuous loop (Figure 5.5).

By engagement in peer discussion linked to scholarly literature, the participant's developing personal experience is triangulated against, and enters into dynamic tension with, the experience of peers and the relevant scholarship; this provides alternative perspectives that support critical reflection.

The conceptual underpinning of this model of reflection is rooted in constructivism, the learning theory which also underpins research and argues that you cannot simply give others your understanding of an area – the student must constructively engage to build their own understanding. Moreover, social constructivism argues that in building complex understandings, an essential role can be played by peer collaboration to promote reflective development. This links to Schon's (1991) notion of the reflective practitioner and to the identification of two sorts of professional reflection – reflection-on-action that occurs after the event, and reflection-in-action: 'the idea that professionals engage in reflective conversations with practical situations, where they constantly frame and reframe a problem as they work on it, testing out their interpretations and solutions' (Calderhead & Gates, 1993: 1).

Cowan takes the Kolbian model one stage further when he expands on Schon's discrimination between reflection-in-action and reflection-on-action. He argues that there is also reflection-for-action, and that in between each stage different reflecting skills are required.

This well-known model of reflection in action, on action and for action can help us to identify three sets of questions that prompt these different types of reflection (see Figure 5.6).

Reflection and maturity

Moon reminds us that the ability to reflect may depend upon maturity (thus introducing the whole person into this generally more depersonalised approach). She gives examples of students work and approves of those that:

- Show evidence of an internal dialogue and self-questioning
- Take into account the views and motives of others and consider these against their own
- Recognise how prior experience, thoughts (their own and others) can interact with the production of their own behaviour
- Show clear evidence of standing back from the event

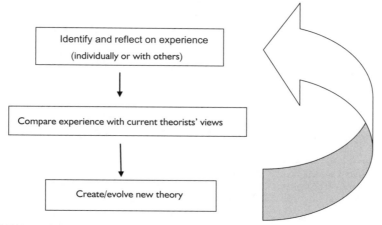

Figure 5.5 A model of reflection

- The student helps themself to learn by splitting off the reflective process from the points they want to learn (e.g. by an asterisk system)
- Show recognition that the personal frame of reference can change according to the emotional state in which it is written, the acquisition of new information, the review of ideas and the effect of time passing. (Moon 2004: 209)

There is a balance that needs to be struck between the need for guidance against the desirability of students doing their own thinking without too much help. How much help to give must be influenced by level of study and prior experience, together with the goals of the course.

Becoming a reflective professional is about including some of these processes in our daily lives. Moon also recommends keeping a reflective diary as a way of capturing incidents and focusing our attention on our own professional development. Increasingly requirements for continuing professional development (CPD) are asking for evidence of reflection and subsequent professional growth. Some students using qualitative research techniques will already be keeping such a diary and will need to incorporate evidence from it in their final thesis. Box 5.3 summarises a range of questions that can be addressed to students writing research diaries. They will help students develop their metacognitive skills.

This chapter ends with two quotations from supervisors which demonstrate the centrality of critical thinking to teaching postgraduate students:

> ... an outstanding student, is someone (who) really has a lot of get up and go and I think an average student is someone who just really needs a lot of help to try and question ... What we teach fundamentally

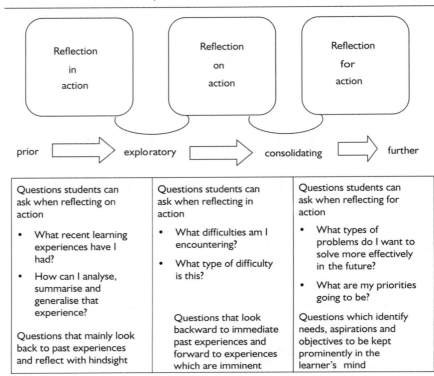

Figure 5.6 Questions to support reflection in, on and for action (after Cowan 2008: 53)

in graduate school is how to solve a problem, research methods and theoretical tools and methods and how to take a problem and solve it or address it in a convincing way; we teach them how to do things, how to answer questions. (Soft applied).

What we don't really teach people in a systematic way is how to recognise the questions and to frame them in tractable ways. That's really the difference between a good and an average student. They all have the methods, research methods and skills and the literature and you know have … the ambitions for writing a thesis, for example, but the really good students are the ones that can go that next step and actually can formulate interesting problems. Those are the ones that really stand out because those are the ones that are going to really advance the field. The ones that have sensitivity in respect to a question … that is something that you don't teach in any courses. It's like my seminars, that's what I talk to students about. OK that is what I praise them for when they do that, I feel I have to give them a lot of affirmation, when they take that

Box 5.3 Helping students to develop their metacognitive skills

Encourage them to keep a research diary to:

1 Show evidence of an internal dialogue and self-questioning, especially questioning why they are doing this research now.
2 Seek to understand the views and motives of others and consider these against their own.
3 Recognise how prior experience (their own and that of others) can affect their research.
4 Demonstrate that they can stand back from the event.
5 Identify their learning points and then examine how they learned them.
6 Recognise that the personal frame of reference can change according to the emotional state in which it is written, the acquisition of new information, the review of ideas and the effect of time passing.

step, because that's really the unusual part, the part where I kind of stand up and applaud. (Soft applied)

The stages of development that were first identified by Perry (1970) have spawned profound research about how we can expect students to move in their beliefs about knowledge (epistemological development) and embrace an ontological perspective (become and embody whatever philosophical position they decide to espouse). This element of how critical thinking can lead to transformation is further explored in the next chapter on emancipation.

Further reading

Barnett, R. (2009) 'Knowing and becoming in the higher education curriculum'. *Studies in Higher Education.* 34.4: 429–440.
Donald, J. G. (2002) *Learning to Think.* San Francisco, CA: Jossey-Bass.
Hay, D. (2007) 'Using concept maps to measure deep, surface and non-learning outcomes'. *Studies in Higher Education.* 32.1: 39–57.
Wisker, G. and Robinson, G. (2009) 'Encouraging postgraduate students of literature and art to cross conceptual thresholds'. *Innovations in Education and Teaching International.* 46.3: 317–330.

Chapter 6

Enabling emancipation

The emancipatory approach: an introduction

In this approach the academic wants the student to find their own direction and values and to decide to apply them to their research. They offer support and challenge at appropriate times and are careful not to impose their own agenda. Supervision meetings and group work will be characterised by the academic offering and seeking information and seeking the student's opinions. Occasionally they may decide to allow a student to fail at a particular task and then help the student to identify learning from that experience.

Supportive environments and emancipatory knowledge

Habermas argues that emancipatory knowledge means that social constraints must be made apparent and a supportive environment is required. He proposed that there is:

> A basic human interest in rational autonomy and freedom which issues in a demand for the intellectual and material conditions in which non-alienated communication and interaction can occur.
>
> (Carr & Kemmis 1986: 135–136)

The academics' role in enabling personal development can be seen in several ways. Firstly it needs to be considered in the context of emancipation – the academic who works within this aspect of the framework will be acting as a non-directive mentor who offers challenge and support but who is not seeking to guide the student in any overall direction apart from that of personal growth. Emancipation here has a very different objective to enculturation – typically the academic who is working within an emancipatory framework will not be seeking to keep their student within their discipline, whereas this will be a prime objective for the academic who is working within the enculturation framework. The following quotation illustrates some different views, and how views change over time, about what constitutes an acceptable career path for students; we can see the supervisor moving from an enculturation approach to emancipation.

> I had a year when a lot of students all suddenly decided to take very different careers and one student who had been an undergraduate with me and he was really sharp and I managed to convince him to stay as a post doc. And I thought he would be just the perfect faculty member and then when he announced to me he was going to go into Management Consulting, I was, you know, totally flabbergasted. I was shocked and, you know, I worked a little bit on him. I tried to say you should really go into academia, you should go into academia. You know, then I realised that he had his mind set. I remember some colleagues of mine coming up to me and saying, 'What, you are letting him go into Management Consulting – that's horrible', because they were very pleased with him as well. Some of them had been on his defence committee, and you know, and had the same view of him as I had. But I've learnt to respect peoples' career choices. I realise that not everybody can become a professional physicist and it's good to have people who are good at physics in other careers. It speaks well for the discipline. So I've totally changed my opinion now. I … if a student says 'I want to do this, I want to do that' in effect, you know, I … I start talking about careers early on. (Hard pure)

This chapter will look at mentoring as an emancipatory approach to working with postgraduate students. However, before we do that, a word about another two aspects of encouraging personal development: a discussion about what personal development planning can be and about what enquiry-based learning is and how it fits with other active learning approaches.

Defining personal development planning

An alternative way of looking at personal development can be through the lens of creating independent learners, citizenship and employability. In the UK, personal development in higher education is now considered in the context of the Dearing Report (1997) where it was argued that all university graduates at all levels should have access to personal development planning (PDP). What PDP should consist of was not clearly defined.

Whilst the UK national Quality Assurance Agency (QAA) have defined personal development planning in higher education, there is no universally recognised definition of what PDP really is (Brennan & Shah 2003). In the UK, universities were asked to develop progress files: 'a means by which students can monitor, build and reflect upon their personal development' (Dearing 1997).

The QAA guidelines state that PDP is concerned with learning in a holistic sense (both academic and non-academic) and a

> process that involves self-reflection, the creation of a personal record, planning and monitoring progress towards the achievement of personal objectives. (QAA 2001)

The guidelines also give statements about the intended purpose of PDP, i.e. to enable students to become more effective, independent and confident self-directed learners, to understand how they are learning, to relate their learning to a wider context and to improve their general skills for study and career management.

In Australia, at the University of Sydney, research has been carried out on graduate attributes. They have included scholarship, lifelong learning and global citizenship as their desired attributes. (See Barrie 2004, 2006, and the University of Sydney Graduate Attributes Project.) More recently in Australia, attention has focused on enabling research students to identify, articulate and develop the skills and attributes that they already have. This enabling approach is particularly appropriate for experienced, mature students but it demands of the research supervisor the ability to encourage the research student to consider and reflect on the processes they are participating in (Cumming & Kiley 2009).

In a research-led university in the UK, PDP was defined it as falling into three slightly different separate subgroups:

1 Learning, research and scholarship
2 Employability and engagement with society and
3 Personal and communication skills.

Each level of academic study had different learning objectives and course and module leaders had to be able to demonstrate that their students were achieving at least one objective in each sub-group (Burden & Lee 2006).

Creating an emancipatory environment through using enquiry-based learning

At an undergraduate level, the attitude that would be taken to course design within this approach could be to embrace enquiry-based learning (EBL). Enquiry-based learning engages the teacher initially as a guide and later as a collaborator, it encourages students to become actively involved in designing the questions, researching and constructing knowledge. It is a process of learning which includes (but is more than) using research and study skills. Ideally it is holistic (and not limited to cognition) and offers opportunities for creativity. Because it is so different from a didactic approach to teaching, it requires different learning outcomes and assessment strategies; it is often a useful part of the process to engage the students in co-designing the assessment criteria.

Designing enquiry-based learning modules is appropriate when we want to

- equip students with transferable skills of enquiry for an increasingly complex world
- work with transdiscipline/multi-discipline issues of constructed knowledge (including addressing the theory–practice gap), ethical dimensions, at the interface of human/technical working
- enhance engagement.

Whilst EBL is not a new approach to teaching and learning, it has recently been newly emphasised in universities. Its purpose is to develop transferable skills of enquiry to enable coping with complexity and EBL is now a recognised strand in academic practice; in the UK it attracted £4.5m of government money to fund a new Centre for Excellence in Teaching and Learning (CETL) at Manchester University and several other CETLs have worked on similar themes.

Tosey led an enquiry-based learning project at the University of Surrey which investigated how those who said they were using enquiry-based learning methods actually worked in practice. He argued that there are five key dimensions to EBL; and one of those dimensions is that it involves the head, the heart and the hands. His definition is that 'EBL is a process of learning in which the learner has significant influence on or choice about the aim, scope, or topic of their learning. This process of learning draws upon research skills and study skills, but enquiry is not reducible to either research or study' (Tosey & McDonnell 2006: 2).

Hutchings (2007) has described the differences between the traditional teacher and the tutor who focuses on enquiry-based learning in the following way. He argues that the traditional teacher provides materials, sets the boundaries and teaches in a tutor centred manner. In contrast the EBL tutor will facilitate learning by establishing target learning outcomes and providing triggers for learning *whilst the students* collectively examine the problem; decide on the areas requiring more research; conduct the research; collate the information and re-examine their learning.

The root of the word facilitator comes from the latin *facilis* which means 'capable of being done'. It is thus something which is capable of being done, and therefore the facilitator's role is to create the conditions under which a task may be effectively carried out. It is the opposite of to define, to limit or to close down (Gregory 2006b).

This is an approach to designing learning activities which is part of a suite of active learning approaches but it is less directive than problem-based learning where students work on solving a problem pre-defined by the teacher. One way of looking at different types of active learning is portrayed in Figure 6.1.

The three terms problem-based learning; action learning and enquiry-based learning are widely used, and frequently muddled up, so it is worth spending a little time disaggregating them.

The three terms are all members of the same family in that they involve the student in active learning. But they are different in the amount of control that the teacher exerts over the agenda. In this sense I believe that problem-based learning and action learning are polar opposites.

In problem-based learning the academic will set the students the problem. For example students will be asked to 'mend, and if possible improve this toaster' rather than be told in a transmission-based manner that 'today we are going to study the flow of electricity through metals ...'. True problem-based learning will encourage exploratory research; it will encourage students to apply a variety of interpretative contexts in order to allow them to develop their own sense of which is appropriate and it will encourage an active and creative engagement of the students with the creative potential of the subject (Hutchings 2007).

PROBLEM-BASED LEARNING

Academic sets the problem and the process

Group solves the problem

ENQUIRY-BASED LEARNING

Academic and learner collaborate in solving a teacher-set problem

Academic provides hands-on help and encourages a

holistic process

ACTION LEARNING

Learners may define the problem

Academic may ensure equity for all participants

Figure 6.1 Different approaches to active learning

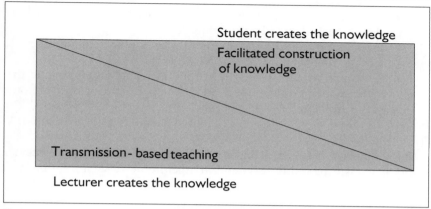

Figure 6.2 The overlap between transmission-based teaching and facilitated construction of knowledge

In action learning participants take ownership of formulating the problem. Beaty describes action learning as:

> A continuous process of learning and reflection, supported by colleagues with an intention of getting things done. Through action learning individuals learn with and from each other by working on real problems and reflecting on their own experiences.
>
> (Beaty 2003: 4)

A common method of the facilitator 'controlling' the action learning group is to ensure that each participant has the same amount of time to present their story (Weinstein 1999: 157).

Enquiry-based learning moves the academic away from their role as being the fount of all knowledge to becoming a knowledgeable equal.

In reality, between enculturation and emancipation there is an overlap and blurring which is described in Figure 6.2. For the purposes of analysis we are looking at them as separate approaches.

Kahn and O'Rourke (2004) have produced a useful short guide to understanding enquiry-based learning, and in it they suggest:

> Enquiry-Based Learning (EBL) is used here as a broad umbrella term to describe approaches to learning that are driven by a process of enquiry. We can outline some of the characteristics of EBL as follows:
> * Engagement – with a complex problem or scenario – that is sufficiently open-ended to allow a variety of responses or solutions.
> * Students direct the lines of enquiry and the methods employed.

- The enquiry requires students to draw on existing knowledge and to identify their required learning needs.
- Tasks stimulate curiosity in the students, encouraging them to actively explore and seek out new evidence.
- Responsibility falls to the student for analysing and presenting that evidence in appropriate ways and in support of their own response to the problem.

(Kahn & O'Rourke 2004: 2)

This boundary between being in control as an academic and being a co-inquirer was explored by Rowland in a field note reflecting on his own teaching.

> (several meetings later) The Group were discussing how they would be presenting their portfolios for assessment. I felt somewhat awkward in this discussion because it seemed to force me back into a tutorly role, rather than one of an equal collaborator in the enquiry. I suspect some of them felt the same. They wanted me to say something about how I would assess their work. I said that, as with the last module, I would read it and give them each a page or two of my comments, which could then be the subject of personal tutorials later.
>
> I then reminded them of a conversation we had had several meetings ago when they talked about feedback as a means of promoting growth, or as a means of control. I asked whether they felt that my feedback to them on the portfolios would be viewed as a form of control or growth. This led to a valuable discussion, which also served to deal with some of the tensions which I – and I believe they – felt about my assessing their work. It also led to several references about how it must feel to be a student being assessed.
>
> (Rowland 2000: 59)

Box 6.1 combines all of the threads discussed in this section and poses nine questions that the academic can ask themselves to check how effective they are in managing enquiry-based learning in the curriculum.

Working with small groups: the psychosocial model of facilitation

This model assumes that where students come together voluntarily, learning will happen automatically if the relationships within the group are positive. The father of non-directive therapy, Rogers (1983) suggested that facilitators needed six role sets: they set the initial mood of the group, elicit and clarify individual and group purposes, regard themselves as a flexible

Box 6.1 Self assessment questions – are you facilitating enquiry-based learning?

1 Do you demonstrate that you are also an EBL learner?
2 Do you create conditions for creativity (create frameworks for learning that are appropriate for the context, student ability and experience)?
3 Do you agree ground rules?
4 Do you prepare students for this way of learning?
5 Do you facilitate discussion and student engagement in a non-directive way?
6 Do you monitor student progress and offer encouragement and support?
7 Do you help students to evaluate their learning, e.g. through collaborative development of criteria?
8 Do you assess group learning?
9 Do you provide a safety net to enable student development?

resource, respond to both intellectual and emotional expressions from the group, share their personal feelings and work to recognise and accept their own limitations.

There are many other models of group functioning and group relationships which focus on the interpersonal dynamics of an interactive group. One such model is called FIRO-B (an abbreviation for Fundamental Interpersonal Relations Orientation – Behaviour). This model was devised by Will Schutz (1984, 2004); it identifies the key motivators that drive behaviour and help transform a disparate group of individuals into a cohesive productive group. The model helps individuals to discover how their needs for participation, influence and closeness can be contributing to or detracting from their success as a learning group.

Schutz argues that if the key concepts of inclusion, control and openness are not attended to, group members will stop learning because they will feel either ignored, humiliated or rejected or fight for more recognition (inclusion) influence and attention to their (emotional) needs.

Another psycho-social model concentrates on looking at the intent behind the intervention. Heron (1999, 2001) has written at length about facilitation and the six categories of interventions that he has identified. Like Egan (2002), he intended his six-category intervention analysis to be used in one-to-one situations, but it is a rich analysis and much is transferable to identifying skills for group facilitation and for enhancing supervision skills in all the approaches.

The core of his argument is that the skilled facilitator makes an intervention competently, free from any hidden agendas, and knows exactly what the intent is behind their intervention. Unskilled facilitators are at risk of making manipulative, perverted or degenerate interventions.

Making interventions purely, and constantly being aware of our intentions is a lifelong quest. Heron tries to help us by dividing interventions into those that he calls 'facilitative' and 'authoritative'.

Facilitative interventions are those where the practitioner is seeking to enable the student to become more autonomous. Authoritative interventions are where the practitioner (facilitator) takes responsibility for and on behalf of the student. It is a positivist stance and is about raising consciousness, guiding behaviour and giving instructions.

It is easy to see from the above list that the skilled facilitator/academic teacher will need to be psychologically self aware to understand their intentions when making any intervention. According to Heron, all categories are neutral in that if they are operated competently, one is no better than another. His rider is that the facilitator must always be working from an underlying supportive attitude with students.

Along with other writers, Heron (1999) has also looked at group processes. He identifies three models of facilitating: hierarchical, co-operative and autonomous. Within each mode there are six different dimensions: planning, meaning-making, confronting, feeling, structuring and valuing.

For Heron some of the goals of facilitation are that the student will be able to direct and develop themselves, make informed judgements, be emotionally competent and self aware. He identifies a hierarchy of facilitator 'states' (this is a way of identifying the level of 'presence' that the facilitator has): at level 1 the facilitator shows no interest or empathy in participant or subject matter – submerged in his/her own internal anxiety and concerns; at level 2 the facilitator is fascinated by the subject, their own distress, or the participant, to the exclusion of all else; whereas at level 3 the facilitator's attention is distracted, goes off in directions irrelevant to work at hand. At level 4 the facilitator displaces their own distress, confusion or conflict on to the student by attacking, withdrawing, blaming, denial, complaining etc. At level 5 there is greater control of attention energy: some attention for the task in hand while the remainder is buried, displaced, distracted etc. At level 6 there is full attention directed to the task in hand encompassing both own and participants' needs; at level 7 that full attention also encompasses past and future to create context and at level 8 metacognitive skills are at work, the facilitator being able to be fully engaged but also working at the disidentified witness/monitoring level.

Levels 6–8 will create an environment that is the most meaningful for the learner and probably exhausting but rewarding for the facilitator.

Working one-to-one: the research supervisor as a mentor

Pearson and Kayrooz (2004) argue that research supervision is a facilitative process requiring support and challenge. It involves providing educational tasks and activities which include progressing the candidature, mentoring, coaching the research project and sponsoring student participation in academic practice. This is similar to the journey conception identified by Brew (2001). A defining question which can mark the line between the facilitation and enculturation approach is: 'how much responsibility should the student or the academic take for arriving at the destination?'

The importance of journeying from the known and students discovering and testing knowledge for themselves was highlighted by Carl Rogers (1967):

> I have come to feel that the only learning which significantly influences behaviour is self-discovered, self-appropriated learning. ... Such self-discovered learning, truth that has been personally appropriated and assimilated in experience, cannot be directly communicated to another ... When I try to teach, as I do sometimes, I am appalled by the results, which seem a little more than inconsequential, because sometimes the teaching seems to succeed. When this happens, I find that the results are damaging. It seems to cause the individual to distrust his own experience, and to stifle significant learning. Hence I have come to feel that the outcomes of teaching are either unimportant or hurtful.
>
> As a consequence, I realise that I am only interested in being a learner ... I find that one of the best, but most difficult ways for me to learn, is to drop my own defensiveness, at least temporarily, and to try to understand the way in which (the other person's experience) seems and feels to them.
>
> (Rogers 1967: 276–277)

In this second paragraph Rogers is describing the importance of empathy in the relationship, but we need to be aware that non-directive therapy (or teaching) can never totally live up to its name. As the therapist (teacher) chooses the questions he or she asks, so the facilitator has an influence over the type of knowledge base to be covered.

Mentoring is a powerful concept in this arena (Pearson & Brew 2002). There is much literature on mentoring in general and facilitation skills in particular (Lee 2006, 2007). The mentor is usually seen as a non-judgemental adviser. Mentoring builds upon Rogers' belief that self experience and self-discovery are important facets of learning (Morton-Cooper & Palmer 2000) and it involves acknowledging that adults can move from being dependent to being self-directed, accumulate experiences and create a biography from which they can learn and can change. The expected movement is from needing to acquire knowledge and being subject centred to becoming more performance centred. The objective is the application of experience and the development of sound critical thinking abilities.

A mentor can be primary or secondary (Kram 1985, Freeman 1998). The secondary mentor has much more of a businesslike relationship with their mentee. They concentrate on providing support for career development, they can suggest projects, help to solve work-based problems, provide coaching where they have particular skills and might actively promote their mentee where they think it could be helpful.

The primary mentor can provide a more profound experience and some academics will feel that this goes beyond what they are expected to do. When an emotional bond is developed the mentee is deemed to have a primary mentor and the approach to supervision is moving towards the next category in the framework – building a relationship of friendship. The strength of the primary mentor is that they provide acceptance and confirmation that the mentee is worthwhile and this leads to personal empowerment. They can help the mentee to learn from a variety of life experiences as well as planning and rehearsing future encounters.

Secondary mentors are obviously easier to find. Sometimes a relationship starts with more functional, secondary mentoring expectations, and goes on to become extremely fundamental for both parties.

Emancipation as a supervisory process implies both support and challenge. It is also a process which allows and supports personal transformation; the potential for the research process to be transformative becomes clear when we look at the prerequisites for transformative learning; it is perceived as requiring critical reflection and a disorienting dilemma (Mezirow 1991, Taylor 2007).

This element of enabling students to cope, whilst also giving them information which may disturb and disorientate them, can also cause conflicts between academics. Some may believe that this period of disorientation needs to be deeply experienced if the student is to understand it, others may feel that this is cruel and unnecessary and the dilemma can usually be resolved through discussion about the place of disorientation in higher education. If members of the academic team can understand and respect (and sometimes amend) the position of others, the student stands to gain.

'What do you want to learn?' Herman and Mandell (2004) recommend that every mentor asks this powerful question at each meeting and every mentee prepares themselves to answer that same question before the meeting. The emancipatory supervisor could choose to begin a meeting with research students with a similar question. Asking a student (or a group of students) to focus on this every time they meet develops metacognitive abilities and helps the movement towards becoming an independent learner.

The research supervisor as mentor will want the student to understand what motivates them:

I want to know what their connection is with the research, why are they asking this question. For student x it was not external research, it was quite existential. (Soft applied)

Acknowledging the dependency stage, academics said,

I try to get them to admit and confront their problems. (Soft pure)

I act as a bridge between the knowledge and the student and eventually they don't need me. (Hard pure)

Again there is acknowledgement that this is only a beginning:

I am always waiting for that epiphany moment when they say 'no I don't agree'. (Hard applied)

You get a lot of satisfaction, you have facilitated that growth in them. (Soft pure)

The lack of need for control is what makes this category differ from enculturation:

At the start you know a little bit more than them, but not much. Your job as a supervisor is to get them to the stage of knowing more than you. (Hard applied)

I want it to have changed how they see the world. (Soft applied)

Very few of my students are doing it for an academic career, they want the intellectual rewards. I want my students to have had adequate challenge and support to get that. (Soft applied)

The academic as mentor needs to 'hold the space' for the student. Supervision is also emancipatory in the sense that it involves developing motivational strategies that help students to increase self-efficacy, i.e. confidence in their ability to learn and progress in their writing. There is evidence that when students experience success in managing their writing effectively, their self-efficacy increases, and self-efficacy has been linked to improved attainment in academic writing (Zimmerman, Bandura & Martinez-Pons 1992).

There is a role for failure. As Bandura (1994) noted, if students experience only easy successes they have no opportunity to develop resilience and emerge stronger through adversity. The extract from an interview below demonstrates this point in practice.

I had a student working on a project, that I considered very, very good and she was somebody who ... was probably better at analysis of data than collecting data and she kept collecting data that just didn't make sense ... to us. It was becoming clear that she was not a great person in the lab, so I thought, oh well ... maybe she is not that good an experimentalist, you know, we will have to teach her how to do things. But it wasn't that at all, it was just there was something there, in her data that we were just completely missing. We really had to have thought totally, totally differently and we missed it so I feel guilty about missing it because a group in (another major university), in fact, didn't miss it ... and as soon as they reported their findings we understood ... exactly why ... it wasn't working and, you know, she spent nearly two years doing that ... . And this frustrated her to no end, she was really unhappy and bitter about it. And yet I think it made her a much stronger scientist, and then she started doing things, other things ok ... we just started doing things that worked more easily and she got her degree ... , she was there for 6 years, I think, 2 years of her experience was unpleasant, because she wasn't getting things to work. She came with two of her peers, and came the same year who were just getting everything to work. So she was bound to feel why are things not working? ... But in the long run, you know, I don't feel that badly, although I recognise and I do feel it myself, the frustrations are something we all have to go through. You know, we have to learn how to deal with this kind of frustration, because she is going to face it again. If she takes a path in her career in science. And, I ... fully expect her to appreciate that in the long run even though she didn't, she doesn't now. (Hard pure).

A good mentor will know how to help a student learn from difficult experiences and from failure, Clutterbuck and Ragins argue that the quality of the relationship is more important than whether the relationship is formal or informal. (Clutterbuck & Ragins 2002: 45) and this observation demonstrates yet another blurring of the boundaries, in this case between the emancipatory and relationship approaches.

Mentoring also has its dark side, the uncritical mentee faced with an untrained mentor who is burdened with a lack of self-awareness can be a problem. Berglass (2002) has shown how some coaches 'gain a Svengali-like hold over both the executives they train and the CEOs they report to' (p. 91). Darling (1985) coined the term 'toxic mentors' and these include avoiders, destroyers and criticisers who would take unfair advantage of their mentees. Egoists could be added to the list. This begins to explain another necessity for training in supervision: academics need to be particularly aware of the dangers of mentoring over issues that they have not fully resolved themselves, the boundaries need to be clearly thought through. The mentoring academic does not direct, they 'midwife' the project, dissertation or thesis and it can take some time to understand this position and to develop the skills to perform it.

The limits of the role of mentoring for the research student

A mentor can be an appropriate significant other who can provide honest guidance, support and challenge at the right moments for their mentee. Thus the true mentor does not have to be a 'supervisor', and should not be a line manager or an assessor. (Various organisations and professions have appropriated the term 'mentor' and applied it in these ways.) The quality of a pure mentoring relationship is one which is voluntarily entered into and where there is already a positive regard on both sides. It can provide a profound learning experience (for both sides). The research supervisor can take a mentoring approach, but because of their organisational role and obligations they may have to manage the conflict of interest that is inherent in adopting this approach.

When is mentoring most beneficial?

Critical incidents can provide rich food for reflection, but often past experiences can be used as a gateway to reveal more about present concerns. The experienced mentor will spot such opportunities to open doors and reveal trends or illuminate blind spots (Egan 2002). Mentoring is used to help mentees into a new role or organisation, to fast-track their development, to develop cross-cultural awareness, to aid coping with managing change, to help manage the conflict between the professional role, patient autonomy and organisational demands, to help manage the cloak of defence against emotion and to help those who are seeking explanations of their own perceived inadequacy (Morton-Cooper & Palmer 2000). However it is worth emphasising that mentoring is for the well, not for the sick.

What do the mentor and mentee gain?

The mentee obviously benefits from this relationship when it is at its most productive. They learn where to spend their time most effectively, they can learn how to cope with organisations more productively and get more job satisfaction (Murray & Owen 1991).

Outside a salaried structure, most mentors undertake this work without seeking or expecting payment but they gain considerable other benefits. They enjoy keeping in touch with others' feelings and experiences, many feel a sense of parental pride; they learn from the relationship, too, and can become more effective academics as a result.

Separating

The mentoring relationship usually ends at some point often because the period of study is completed but sometimes there is a problem with the ending. An unaware mentor can 'cling on' and the mentee can experience a sensation of wanting to escape and reclaim their life. Regular reviews are necessary in advance to establish when the formal mentoring relationship will close, then a friendship or working relationship might continue, but it would be different. It is easier to mark the separation by meeting in a different place, or agreeing to do something different at a final session.

Learning as a transformative experience

It is possible to argue that *all* learning is transformative, but there is a fundamental type of learning which transforms the framework within which the student operates, the way they see themselves and the world, which is often at the heart of the postgraduate student's experience.

For the purposes of this book I am defining a transformative experience as an experience which enables the learner to approach their world in a different and more positive way and which changes (or transforms) the learner in its wake. Mezirow (1991) refers to this as 'a meaning perspective' (p. 46) and reminds us that the sociologist Erving Goffman used the term 'frame' to refer to a shared definition of a situation that organises and governs social interaction. 'Reframing' has been used as a way of demonstrating that this shared definition can be developed.

Mezirow suggested that there were a set of phases that people go through when they experience transformation, and they usually start with a problem (a disorientating dilemma), and the person moves through a problem-solving process to a place of reintegration.

Senge (1990) takes these boundaries one stage further when he describes this transformative learning process as 'metanoia'. 'To grasp the meaning of metanoia is to grasp the deeper meaning of learning, for learning also involves a fundamental shift of mind' (p. 10).

He links this ability to learn individually through groups to dia-logos (to the Greeks dia-logos meant a free flowing of meaning through a group allowing the group to discover insights not attainable individually'). He also links this on to the concept of the learning organisation (and thereby makes explicit the premise that enabling staff to pursue the transformative agenda will enhance the employing organisation).

Mezirow takes the question of how to understand knowledge firmly back to the philosopher. This would lead the facilitator to ask 'in how many ways can we disprove this' (after Popper 1963), and 'can we make explicit what we are taking for granted' (looking for tacit knowledge). 'Popper and the transformation theorists agree that our efforts to understand the world generate the continuous testing of our most fundamental assumptions' (Mezirow 1991: 41).

Brooks studied 29 managers who were identified as critically reflective by their peers. She identified what she called first and second order thinking. First order thinking involved empathically taking another person's or group's perspective and listening to intuition. Second order thinking included perspective taking, monitoring thought processes, gathering information and using analytical processes (Brooks 1989 in Mezirow 1991: 181). Here we begin to see the skills required of the transformative facilitator: they are a mix of the psycho-social and critical thinking skills combined at a high level. Tosey (2008) reminds us of the link to knowledge and meaning at the imaginal level (see also Chapter 5) and argues that it is at this deep, metaphorical level, that we need to access our understanding if transformation, as Mezirow sees it, is to take place. This discussion forces us to acknowledge another blurred boundary in the framework and to ask the question: is it possible to be an effective mentor without critical thinking?

The research supervisor can enact a mentoring role in two ways: the obvious role is in being responsible for supervising students; a less obvious but equally important role is to act as a mentor for probationary staff, co-supervisors and new supervisors. Some quality assurance procedures require that a doctoral supervisor must have been a co-supervisor one, two or more times before they can become a primary supervisor (Code of Practice for Research Degrees 2000). Mentoring a colleague requires similar skills of knowing when to support and when to challenge: it is also helpful if there is a shared neutral language to debate the purpose of the research process and the different approaches that can be adopted. Members of a supervisory team can achieve this by all completing the questionnaire in Table 8.16.

A mentoring relationship is inherently a professional one; in the next chapter we explore the other side of this line, where the relationship between academic and student becomes more personal and altruistic, energising and rewarding for both parties. yet still stays within appropriate boundaries.

Further reading

Clutterbuck, D. and Ragins, B. R. (2002) *Mentoring and Diversity*. Oxford: Butterworth Heinemann.

Heron, J. (1999) *The Complete Facilitator's Handbook*. London: Kogan Page.

Heron, J. (2001) *Helping the Client*. London: Sage.

Mezirow, J. (1991) *Transformative Dimensions of Adult Learning*. San Francisco, CA: Jossey-Bass.

Chapter 7

Creating a relationship

The relationship approach: an introduction

In this approach teaching and supervision will be characterised by friendship. The academic and student will anticipate and normally avert unnecessary conflict. Problems will be solved with goodwill, and overt rationalisation will not always need to be expressed for either party to do what is requested. Appropriate boundaries will be observed but the student and academic may introduce each other to friends and family.

The quality of a relationship between teacher and student has been recognised as an important, even the most important, determinant of student satisfaction with teachers (Harkin 1998, Smith 1997, Carson 1996). Poor relationships have been linked to poor completion rates (Taylor & Beasley, 2005: 69) so in this context we are seeking what Clarkson (1995) called a 'working alliance', a productive alliance around a shared task.

Friendship is an important element in this approach. Aristotle argued that friendship is essential 'nobody would choose to live without friends, even if he had all the other good things' (Thomson 2004: 258). He divides friendships into those of utility (which the other four aspects of the framework in this book could fall largely into), erotic friendships (which cross a boundary of acceptability in working with and assessing students) and perfect friendships.

> Perfect friendships are based on goodness and are obviously the most valuable; here friends care more about the other person than they care about themselves. Moreover it means liking the other person for what he/she is, not for any incidental quality that they might possess such as beauty. Such friends have similar attributes and such friendships only occur after a long while. The relationship needs time to develop. According to Aristotle you cannot get to know each other until you have eaten the proverbial quantity of salt together. This apparently is a medimnos or one and a half bushels. In other words, the friends need to share many meals together, mealtimes traditionally being times of social

chatting, anecdote-telling and story swapping. Finally there are few truly good friendships for there are few truly good people.

(Vardy & Grosch 1999: 32/33)

Macfarlane (2009) introduces Aristotle's moral virtues into this arena when he calls for (amongst others) courage, temperance, liberality, magnificence, friendliness and wittiness. He points out that the twin pressures on academics of the massification of higher education and the pressures to research combine to put virtue and ethics under greater strain. If we are to develop a holistic approach to supervising the student who does research, the existence of this pressure explains why it is so important to explore this final strand of the framework: developing the relationship.

The need for a positive relationship was demonstrated again by Ives and Rowley (2005) in their interviews of supervisor/student dyads and in particular in their examination of relationships where there was dissatisfaction, they found that interruptions in the relationship caused students problems. In their work a good relationship did not necessarily imply that friendship was experienced at the beginning of the research process, indeed they suggest that friendship can get in the way of a good supervisory relationship because it might blunt the ability to be critical. 'The power dynamic between supervisor and student makes friendship difficult' (p. 536).

Wisker *et al.*, (2003a, 2003b) argue that emotional intelligence and flexibility play a large part in working with students through to successful completion. Emotional intelligence has become a contested but popular phenomenon in this field. It has been usefully demonstrated that there are four main aspects to emotional intelligence: perceiving and expressing emotion; understanding emotion; using emotion to facilitate thought; and managing emotion in self and others (Salovey & Mayer 1997). Some academics will be naturally more interested in and able to notice emotion in their students than others. The interviews I conducted suggested that this is such a key part of the supervisory process for the student that I recommend that academic teams do give explicit recognition to whoever in the team takes on the greatest responsibility here. One student spoke for many when he said:

The more pastoral support of the supervisors was really important. I remember being surprised at how helpful they were. This was as important in helping me to get through as any intellectual support.

(Student – social sciences)

Part of managing emotion is the ability to manage conflict (Salovey & Mayer 1997).

Academic: I hate conflict. I would resolve any conflict before it even happens, you know. But I've had some other groups come to me, in fact, you know, I have quite a … whenever there a conflict somewhere in my department, the student is sent to me. I'm seen as somebody who can resolve conflict.

Interviewer: *So how do you do that?*

Academic: Well, I just try to rationalise things and, you know, try to see to what extent I can take away the emotions and bring, you know, usually by talking to the students, very occasionally by talking to the superviosr. In really, really bad cases I've taken on a student who did not get along with his or her adviser. (Hard pure)

The literature of coaching and organisational development can help us to understand more here. Morgan (1997: 205–209) suggests that there are five different ways of handling conflict (based on a study of chief executives): avoidance, compromise, competition, accommodation and collaboration. As Harrison (2002) points out, each situation requires an approach appropriate to the situation,

sometimes collaboration will not work; it may be better to go for compromise through negotiation in order to preserve all players' commitment and to move the game forward. Sometimes it may be wise to abandon a chosen course in the interests of making progress on another front.

(Harrison 2002: 121)

The relationship between the academic and the postgraduate student can be a very close one; consequently much time is spent in supervisors' workshops debating how we identify appropriate boundaries. Do we grieve when our student loses a parent or partner? Do we feel their hunger if they do not have sufficient to eat? Do we worry about their health? Academic teams can provide support to the supervisor who is getting 'sucked in' to a relationship, perhaps sharing and reducing the burden. Such a team can also ensure that someone does know if the student is experiencing some kind of trauma. The literature on psychological contracts is derived mostly from organisational development and human resources groups (Rousseau 1995, Guest & Conway 2002, Chartered Institute of Personnel Development (CIPD), Schein 1980).

The professional body for Human Resource management in the UK says:

The phrase 'psychological contract' was first used in the early 1960s, but became more popular following the economic downturn in the early 1990s. It has been defined as '… the perceptions of the two parties, employee and employer, of what their mutual obligations are towards each other' (Guest & Conway 2002). These obligations will often be informal and imprecise: they may be inferred from actions or from what has happened in the past, as well as from statements made by the employer, for example during the recruitment process or in performance appraisals. Some obligations may be seen as 'promises' and others as 'expectations'. The important thing is that they are believed by the employee to be part of the relationship with the employer.

(cipd.co.uk)

Contracts are useful, they free us to act within the terms of a contract without needing to check whether or not we are working within expectations all the time. However (psychological) implied contracts need to be made as explicit as possible for several reasons. Firstly the clarification of expectations means that both parties are likely to work together harmoniously for longer and unexpected violations are less likely to happen. Secondly, when changes happen, the impact on the contract can be fully prepared for.

Contracts take into account the differences in power between the parties. In the supervisory relationship the academic has power over resources, knowledge and expertise, the ultimate power lies in the assessment procedure and there is some residual power in giving references. The student has some power over the academic's need to meet completion targets and other aspects of the academic's reputation. This cannot (yet) be a relationship of equals. Hockey (1996) recommends that explicit contracts should be agreed between student and supervisor, and argues that this is a much-neglected approach.

The healthy relationship requires more than a bald analysis of power over resources. It requires agreement over boundaries and (looking at the literature on coaching) Hawkins (2006) recommends that these boundaries should be explicitly discussed. In negotiating the boundary over confidentiality he recommends a discussion about promising limited confidentiality:

> In negotiating the appropriate confidentiality boundary for any form of supervision, it is inappropriate to say everything is confidential that is shared here, or that nothing here is confidential ... we also give our supervisees the undertaking that we will treat everything they share with us in a professional manner and not gossip about their situation.
>
> (Hawkins 2006: 209)

The student is the more dependent person in the dyad, and this means that the responsibility lies with the academic to take the initiative – at least initially. The interviews demonstrated that a desire to enthuse, encourage, recognise achievement and offer pastoral support were all indicators of a positive relationship. The following quotations include some comments academics made when reflecting on their own experiences as students:

> Research supervision is a very personal thing. It is about relationships. If they don't have the motivation you need to fire the imagination, it is different for different students. (Hard pure)

> I wanted to call my supervisor the moment I solved the tough maths. (Hard pure)

Friendship at an early stage might cause difficulties, but after several years of close contact some academics found it became inescapable and several supervisors mentioned how some of their doctoral students became lifelong friends. There is also a pain associated with the relationship dimension:

> We ended up being good friends, she (my supervisor) was only seven years older than me. (Soft applied)

> My supervisors are lifelong friends. I am still angry with the student who passed and dropped off the end of the earth after five years working together. (Soft applied)

> I wish supervising was more like the critical thinking model – less concerned with the welfare of the student – because when they stab you in the back it would hurt less. I want to make sure they have a good time. (Soft applied)

The part of the relationship approach which fostered independence was characterised by altruism.

> I really think my relationship with my supervisor opened my eyes. It was the character of my supervisor, it went beyond mere mentoring. He was considered unconventional, a maverick ... My supervisor helped me with my writing but never pressed me to publish. (Soft applied)

Within this approach there are also issues relating to gender, caring and sexuality. It was interesting to observe the warmth with which one academic hugged his PhD student on her return from holiday, but the communication was unspoken. Delamont *et al.* (2000) refer to the problems that can arise when sexual relationships are entered into and suggest that the academic should follow the rules suggested by the medical profession in these cases. Two quotations illustrating the gender and caring issues are below, the first one in particular risks gender stereotyping and I include it to warn us about the risks of doing this:

> Women tend to listen more and look at body language, rather than just listen to what is actually being said. 'Everything is fine.' Women are better at caring, for example we will go through the data and then ask 'what's the real problem?' (Hard applied)

It is important that students feel cared for. The father of one of my student's died in their first year. My experience is that there are some students who have a series of problems. When this student arrived he first was so ill he could not attend the induction, then his father died, then his wife went into hospital, then his wife got pregnant and depressed ... children will demand attention ... it all happened to one person, it was traumatic for me too. (Hard applied)

In some cases it is the academic who expects a lifelong relationship and experiences rejection when this does not transpire. Below is an example of an academic's reply, when asked if they knew what their (many) PhD students had gone on to do, they replied:

Oh yes, I know (where they all are). I'm in touch with each and every one of them. So some have gone into industry, some have gone into academic positions and are professors now in a variety of places and a variety of countries. And some have gone into other jobs – from venture capital to management consulting to politics ... so I'm actually proud in different ways of many of them. I could also say the same of some of my post docs too because I keep in touch with people who have been in my group – and my graduates and post docs. ... And I try to coach them in their future career. It doesn't stop, you know, it doesn't stop with them leaving my group and me giving them their PhD degree ... for many of them (I) keep writing letters of recommendation and support for years and years and years. Another one is a professor at xxx university, yes, so they have done well. I've worked very hard on coaching them and helping them to the extent I can because their success eventually, you know, their success eventually reflects on me ... It's a family, an intellectual family. That is how I consider it. (Hard pure)

Another academic mentioned a feeling of rejection and identified it as resulting from the student's transaction-oriented attitude:

The student struggled, passed and then disappeared. If I am going to spend five years supervising someone it is an intensive piece of my life. I want some benefit. I go into it thinking: 'what is it going to be like working with this person for five years' ... I still feel angry with that student for disappearing, it was a transaction not a research relationship, and I need to use my time well. (Soft applied).

The academic operating in the relationship dimension approach is comfortable about sharing their own experience, they are aware of appropriate self-disclosure. In the example below, the academic describes their own career path with students, not out of an enculturation objective, but out of a desire to inform, inspire and share.

> I ask them 'what do you see yourself (doing) in 10 years' and I tell them my career and about the career of others who have been in my group and I've learnt to respect peoples desires and wishes and, you know, I realise that people do best when they are happy about their choice. (Hard pure)

They want more than just a PhD for their students:

> I think a measure of success is turning that PhD into a successful career ... And that successful career can be in industry, it can be in academia, it can be, you know, in a government job, or in a sector outside (my discipline) ... And how do you measure that success? I mean, I don't know exactly how to, how to state that, I mean one of course is: enjoyment of work – public recognition – status of the job and so forth ... And one other thing – *that they remain in touch with me.* [my emphasis]

> ... It varies a lot. I mean there are some, you know, who I'll speak to on a weekly if not monthly basis and there are others I will hear from once every year and again others who I hear from once every 5 years, the last one pains me always because I like to hear from them more often ... It's really because I consider my group to be a family and you know, for years, for 5 years we have worked together intensely and I've supported them intellectually and they have contributed to the groups' success, and they are in a sense a member of a very coherent and tight group. So if they leave and they cut off the communication, yes, I think I, I, I feel bad about that. (Hard pure)

Not every academic would agree that they have a responsibility for the personal life of the student, but some are happy to move beyond the professional boundary:

> Academic: I've had many things from, you know, from relationships that broke up or all kinds of things. Or, you know, culture shock. You know, people coming from Asia and having trouble adapting, to death in family to illness, to serious illness. Umm. Many, and yeah no I've had my share of times where I had to ... I felt being more like being a psychologist than a physicist ... And, you know, I've always, I've always umm overcome that or tried to help by seeing myself more as a friend than adviser ... .and talking and giving my support and advice, and many of my students have sought my advice in these otherwise rather personal matters that, you know, have nothing to do with the PhD.

> Interviewer: Have you ever reached a boundary where you felt this is no longer to do with the PhD?

Academic: Oh yeah of course.

Interviewer: *And felt 'it's not my responsibility'?*

Academic: Well – no, no I do, I think that's an interesting question. I do consider it my – precisely because, you know, it's more than (an academic) relationship. It's more a – as I said before if you consider the group like a family ... then there is more than just the advising, there is the friendship, there is the ... and I had that very nurturing relationship with my adviser back (home). It was very important to me. So, you know, I think the, the intellectual well-being of people depends on their physical and psychological well-being. In other words, if somebody has serious health problems or has serious problems with, lets say, with family or with a significant other, then that will affect their, their work ... unless you support them ... and some of these people, you know, some of the people are, have their family far away ... So if they are facing problems from, you know, cancer to death in the family to, you name it, there's far fewer people to talk to, to lean on ... So, I've always, always lent my support there. (Hard pure)

Creating a healthy relationship

Central to a healthy relationship between student and academic is the issue of trust and a belief in each other's integrity. These are elements which are both reputational and revealed over time. Both student and academic will have reputations to be created and developed, and these are nurtured through a positive regard for each other. In practice this means that a healthy relationship is developed when each keeps their promises. This is true both of the little things (for example: arriving at meetings on time and prepared) and the bigger things (for example: following up on a discussion about putting in a joint grant proposal, belief in the accuracy of results). Hawkins (2006) recommends that breaches in trust are not seen as irremediable, but as opportunities for reflection, learning and relationship-building (p. 210).

The framework highlights the movement from (and between) professional and personal identity (see Table 1.1). This creates a potential conflict because academic goals can conflict with personal goals. Hockey (1996) suggests the following types of postgraduate supervision:

- 'informal'—where the notion of a contractual agreement and trust are of equal importance
- 'comradeship'—where trust is more important than the contract, and
- 'professional'—where the contract becomes more important than trust.

The work of the therapeutic alliance identified two key elements which lead to a positive therapeutic relationship and I am proposing that these are also key in a relationship between academic and student. The first element was that the client perceived the therapist as being helpful, supportive and facilitative and the second was a perception that both were working together as a team with a positive bond (Grenyer 2002).

Managing expectations is key to creating a longer-lasting relationship (Kiley 2006, Murray 2006), and it is important to explore these expectations. Murray identifies a dichotomy in expectations over writing a thesis and explores what happens when students want to learn how to write more concisely and use correct terminology, whereas supervisors' concerns were reported to be about the nature of and evidence for a solid argument. Kiley's questionnaire asks supervisors and students to evaluate how much responsibility the student and the supervisor should each take for the final piece of work. This includes selecting the research topic, identifying the appropriate methodological framework, establishing a programme of study and timetable, acquiring specialist knowledge, arranging regular meetings, checking work is progressing, giving feedback on drafts, offering emotional support and friendship. Kiley says:

> The literature describes at least three forms of expectation which are relevant to this edited paper. The psycho-educational literature describes the self-fulfilling prophecy as a response to one's perceptions of the expectations of others, the socio-psychology literature addresses expectancy value or valence theory, and the management literature discusses expectation of service.
>
> (Kiley 2006: 3)

An experienced supervisor described how they set expectations:

> I always say to them you can go through a love–hate relationship with me. It will probably be more hate than love most of the time, but if we can come out of it at the end still talking to each other, possibly even friends or colleagues in the future, that for me is a good outcome. (Soft applied)

The power of first impressions cannot be ignored in establishing expectations, the first encounter with an academic and the induction of new students is central to creating a good working relationship. The aim is to establish a working alliance where, at the contracting stage, expectations are shared along with hopes and fears. Hawkins recommends completing sentences such as 'My image of successful supervision is … '; 'What I fear happening in supervision is … ' (Hawkins 2006:209).

Box 7.1 Outline induction programme for masters students

Introduction to the institution and key academic and administrative staff
Introduction to working at Masters level:

> The skills of critical analysis
> Referencing for writing journal articles, theses and dissertations
> How to get and use feedback
> What you can expect from teaching methods at Masters level – the role of lectures, case studies, tutorials etc
> Identifying how you learn best and managing time
> An outline of new technologies to be used

Introductory case studies in small groups
Feedback from group work
Experienced postgraduate students form a panel to respond to questions from new students
Social

Starting the group learning

The first few weeks are crucial for the students in establishing our expectations of them, relationships with them and friendships between them. All of these can be achieved expeditiously by working with them as a group early on. A typical introductory programme for a management school is shown in Box 7.1 and a similar programme (which would include more on research methods) can be designed for doctoral students. Some universities have established Graduate Schools, and these introductory programmes can be organised under their auspices.

It is just as important (and easier to forget because the relative informality of the situation means that we can be tempted to make assumptions) that individual research students will need a thorough induction as well. Box 7.2 shows a checklist that a research academic will find useful.

Encouraging students to seek and use feedback

Research students will need to learn to cope with sporadic, sometimes extensive and sometimes difficult feedback so an early discussion about this can be very helpful. You may need to emphasise that feedback asking students to revise the way they are looking at something, does not mean they have failed – it does mean they are being given opportunities to learn. It can be useful to suggest that the student seeks feedback from a range of sources

Box 7.2 Checklist for inducting postgraduate students

1 Establishing expectations
   Have you made clear what you will give your students and what you expect from them?
   Have you ascertained what the student expects from you, and identified any mismatches?
2 Setting study targets
   Have you identified the main milestones?
   Have you agreed an overall timetable?
3 Keeping records and referencing
   Has the student started to summarise, record and correctly reference their work?
   Do they know where to go to get advice on avoiding plagiarism?
4 Enhancing their library skills
   Has the student met the subject librarian?
   Has the student undertaken a library induction?
5 The student as part of an academic team
   Have you introduced your student(s) to other students and members of your academic and administrative team?
   Have they got a list of names, job titles and telephone numbers of key people in the department?
   Have they been invited to use common room facilities?
6 Aiming early for academic writing at postgraduate level
   Have you asked for early pieces of writing and given feedback?
   Have you given the student excellent examples of writing in your discipline?
7 Helping the postgraduate student to overcome isolation
   Has the student met others from their home region and/or from their discipline?
   Have they been introduced and welcomed to postgraduate facilities?
   Are they involved in appropriate conferences?

(post-doctoral researchers, other academics and postgraduate and other students), and does not just rely upon feedback from one academic – this will mean that supervision sessions are more likely to include healthy debate and be more interesting for you. Research students may need to be encouraged to move from a place of compliance to the place of actively constructing their own frames of reference, criteria and boundaries.

The second discussion to have about feedback is much more practical: a discussion about what you are willing to give feedback on (short assignments, essay outlines, draft articles or whole chapters of a thesis?) and how much time they should expect to elapse before it is given. Do you prefer to give feedback in writing or face to face?

The student as part of an academic team

In many universities doctoral students are treated in a similar way to junior academic members of staff, and this is a good way to begin to include them as members of the academic tribe. They have their own desks and equipment, and access to staff common rooms. Masters students and undergraduates may or may not have quite such close access to academics, but they do need to be encouraged to create their own learning communities, and these learning communities need to be nurtured by academic staff. Some academics create such learning groups, and give them some occasional form by suggesting they discuss certain books or journal articles, or invite certain speakers.

Helping the research student to overcome isolation

Isolation, and the fear of isolation, challenges most of us (Grenyer 2002, Hockey 1994). A research student who is a member of a minority ethnic group, living and working for the first time in a new country where the cultural expectations clash with those of the homeland can feel exceptionally lonely, however, domestic students can be isolated too; they can find the environment foreign and be unwilling to challenge an academic intellectually or to ask for help socially. A key for many students' ability to complete their studies is whether or not they find friends and colleagues that they can work and socialise with. The outline induction programme (Box 7.1) can be used to help the formation of these groups. Time spent on the formation of study groups early on in the induction procedure can make all the difference to students being able to maintain momentum during the whole of their studies and an agreed programme of regular tutorials at more frequent intervals in the early stages can also be helpful. Whilst the induction period is a golden opportunity for encouraging the formation of study groups, it is not the only one. Box 7.3 summarises a list of suggestions to encourage group work that can be implemented at any time.

Helping a student to establish their own network

It is not uncommon for students to be muddled about who to go to for different kinds of help. They may have personal tutors, advisors, academic

Box 7.3 Helping students to overcome isolation

Have you:

1 Encouraged small peer groups of students to organise themselves to meet regularly?
2 Involved the department in running research seminars – led by both students and staff?
3 Invited academics and other students to hear research students present their work?
4 Considered starting a journal club, or taking a leadership role in organising one for your department?
5 Held conferences especially aimed at research students?
6 Encouraged students to get involved in wider activities?

tutors, primary or co-supervisors, contract researchers, course directors, programme directors and lecturers.

The induction process should make the varying sources of help obvious but in practice the student will go to whomever they feel that they have a good relationship with, and up to a point this is a key part of the student experience: learning to foster good working relationships with a range of people, and finding out where they can get help for a range of different issues.

At doctoral level it is possible for students to be confused about the role of the primary supervisor. For example: is their role to be the focal point of contact with the student, or is it to mentor the second supervisor? Some of this confusion may be deliberately allowed to continue because an academic is embarrassed to admit that they are themselves being mentored – and therefore might be seen by their student as inexperienced. Other times the primary supervisor might have taken notional responsibility for a large number of students, and not been able to focus on the needs of every individual.

Table 7.1 shows a matrix of topics and people, it can be adapted to include local issues and sources. The intention of this type of matrix is that it will foster a discussion that will prepare students for some of the issues that are going to arise during their studies and enable them to handle some of them independently. It can be used in a variety of different learning situations: as a tool for small group discussions in a lecture theatre or in individual supervisions.

Table 7.1 Draft document for discussion with new research students

	Where should the student go to get help with the following?:						
	Lecturer, Contract Researcher, Post doc Adviser	Supervisor Advisor Personal tutor	Subject librarian	Module leader	Careers/ student support/ counselling/ study support centres	Students union/ peers etc	Administrator/ handbook/ other
Understanding subject matter							
Time management							
Statistics skills							
Academic writing							
Timetable for assignments							
Marking criteria							
Financial advice							
Knowing when to expect feedback							
Which journals to read							
Careers advice							
References for job applications							
Personal development planning							
Advice on referencing							
Teaching work experience							
Placements							
Extensions and appeals							

How far should you go in helping students to manage their finances?

University students are adults and academic staffs are not *in loco parentis*. However, if a doctoral student is being funded as part of a team through a research council or other grant, the university has an obligation to ensure that the student does receive that agreed amount of funding over the required time-span. One third of students in the UK do not expect to complete within the minimum three years (Kulej & Park 2008), and this pattern is repeated across Europe (EUA 2007). It is crucial that a student has planned how to pay fees, meet living and travel expenses and pay any research costs, even if they have been offered a fully funded place. Some students plan to do their writing-up whilst they are working – and some achieve it. However, I am an advocate of writing up as much as they can whilst the research is in process because it usually makes the final task easier.

Most UK universities have student hardship funds, some departments have access to (often strictly limited) funds to support doctoral students and there are some charitable trusts that will help – but all of these take time and planning, so the student who suddenly finds their finances have run out, may be in trouble.

A common source of supplementary funding for postgraduate students is to undertake marking and teaching. This is considered useful preparation for an academic career and can be a positive addition to a CV, but the pay levels for this type of work vary considerably, and supervisors will be keen to ensure that a reasonable balance between paid employment and research time is maintained.

The most predictable source of funding is usually when employers sponsor students who are also their employees: Norway is an example of a European country that regards doctoral students as employees anyway, and supports them as members of staff. Students taking professional or practitioner doctorates may also be supported by employers and there usually is a trade-off between autonomy over the research project and funding. Box 7.4 has some questions which the postgraduate supervisor may want to consider before deciding whether to accept a student.

How do you help the student to frame the research proposal?

The obvious question to ask when a student is trying to frame a research project is: why are you doing this? Whilst most undergraduate and masters students will undertake smaller research projects aimed more at developing their skills as researchers than at discovering or creating new knowledge, all research students will need some intrinsic motivation to ensure they can maintain motivation through a research project.

Box 7.4 Helping students to manage their own finances

1   Is funding assured for the fees and living expenses for the minimum time of study?
2   Has the research project been costed – including travel, books, stationery, software etc?
3   Is the student writing up as much as possible as their research proceeds?
4   If the student is funded by an employer, is the salary realistic?
5   Do you know about your university's student hardship fund and any departmental funds for emergencies?
6   Has the student made suitable plans if the research runs over time?

In some cases it is a deeply held personal motivation to study a topic and thereby create some resolution for a personal dilemma, in other cases it is a means to an end – often a job. There are some students who want to undertake personally risky fieldwork – this can mean travelling to countries where there are unstable political regimes or health risks, and some students want to study issues which they are trying to resolve for themselves, e.g. anorexia, bereavement or sex. There are also students who may want to study techniques or pursue experiments where the academic has some ethical concerns about the long-term application of the findings. In all these cases, where there are practical, emotional and/or ethical dilemmas, the academic has some extremely difficult decisions to make.

Some students will arrive with proposals which should really be fully funded research programmes, where the risks that the researcher is going to take need to be carefully evaluated and planned for, in other cases the research proposal is pre-defined as part of a large programme of research being undertaken by the department, so the academic has a key role in recommending a research proposal that is at the right level, worth doing, not too emotionally involving and that can be completed within a reasonable time. In some cases the academic may need to advise the student that the purpose of this piece of work is to acquire research skills and to gain the award; once they have those skills and that status they might be in a stronger place to pursue heartfelt research agendas.

If the academic has serious ethical concerns about the nature of the research proposal (an extreme concern could be, for example, that the results of the research are going to be used for coercion), then as a supervisor they have the right to withdraw.

It looked like a straightforward piece of research on coaching, when we discovered that it was to be used for compliance and not for empowerment, and the institutional context in which the student was working was unchangeable ... we parted amicably I am pleased to say. (Soft pure)

There is also the possibility of the student using their research to act out unresolved personal issues and this dilemma was discussed by a supervisor who is also a psychotherapist and saw some research students as clients:

> I can think now (of situations, for example) ... where a student has experience of rape and was doing research in rape in marital abuse and it was quite clear that there was a real mess here because the supervisor, in my opinion wasn't addressing this. Actually it was highly inappropriate that the student was doing this, and she was being very, very affected by the material she was getting through. It was compounding it rather than resolving it. You get people doing research as a 'means to salvation' as I sometimes call it (they think: 'if I do this good work then it will all be ok'), and the reality is that what can happen is that you get caught out because you get into a form of collusion with your interviewees or research material, and you lose your sense of boundaries really. If the supervisor is not tuned into that it can be really difficult ... similar can happen with research on eating disorders. It is not always the case but it can happen. (Soft applied)

An academic will need to frame the explanation of any decision to withdraw or recommend a change of approach carefully, and document it thoroughly. Ideally they will be seeking to develop the student's awareness of the values implicit in their work, and the different ways of looking at it, whilst perhaps indicating other (healthier) avenues for further study. All of these aspects can be discussed with your students individually or in groups, and Box 7.5 provides a guide for that discussion.

Box 7.5 Helping students to frame their research proposal

1 Are they well motivated to carry out this piece of research?
2 Is the research at the right level (see level descriptors)?
3 Can they access the relevant data/subjects/participants?
4 Is it practical, ethical and achievable within the time?
5 Is there plenty of spare time for contingencies in the project plan (up to 30%)?
6 Are you able to arrange competent supervision over research methods and content?
7 Have they costed it, is it financially viable?

There is a danger of relationships between student and academic developing without boundaries. Clarkson (1995) calls these 'unfinished relationships' where unresolved issues from the past contaminate the present. An academic might be puzzled by a student whose self-esteem seems continuously low, in spite of the fact that the academic is generous with well-deserved affirmation – it could be that as a child the need for appreciation was not gratified, and this has not been resolved. These problems can happen both ways around: the academic can also have unresolved issues which affect the relationship and this is another area where self-awareness of their own unfinished business can help them to make decisions about whether to carry on or delegate some responsibility to another supervisor.

There are also problems that can arise when the relationship becomes too personal. Clarkson (1995) warns us against personal relationships that become so strong that they are more important than the task. The boundary of dealing with student's personal or family problems was clearly drawn by this supervisor:

> I think we probably say if you have got problems with your family then that is not really a University responsibility. We might point out to them that's the issue (if there are issues around that area), but there is not a lot we can do about it. What we can do, from within the University framework, is to make sure that these issues are acknowledged. (Soft applied)

Supervising through reorganisations

In many universities reorganisations are now a fact of life, and usually great efforts are made to protect research students from the effects of them, but they do lead to turmoil and staff grumbling – which a postgraduate student will probably hear more about than any undergraduate would. The academic team needs to be aware that their research students may lose morale, just as staff do, during these trying times. Since many postgraduate research students are aspiring academics, it would not serve them well to pretend that such problems do not exist but it will help enormously if reassurances can be given about their continued support.

Self-awareness and cultural values

Understanding how we are perceived and being aware of the defensive mechanisms we can employ is a life-long journey, and it is not the purpose of this book to suggest that one needs to be a psychotherapist in order to be a successful supervisor. However working with international students provides an opportunity to understand different cultural values. For example, in some cultures the desire for harmony can be stronger than the desire for honesty (Kiley 2006 and see also Chapter 4) and it is only when we have established a relationship where these different values can be explained and explored that high quality teaching and supervision is likely to take place. Academics can and do learn enormously from international students and both worlds can become richer as a result.

Reputations are also developed through third parties (sometimes called 'gossip'!) and how others view both students and academics will have an effect on the relationship between them. There is a philosophical debate about whether the way one behaves in one arena should be linked to behaviour in another (a discussion which is often had about politicians and the relevance – or otherwise – of their private lives). However the practical outcomes are relevant – an academic with a reputation for being generous or brusque, easy or demanding, will find that their students' expectations affect the quality of the work they produce, so conscious awareness of our own reputations can be helpful to developing emotionally intelligent relationships with students.

A relationship can be developed with the student through feedback on their writing; one academic discussed the problems with a student who was frequently silent:

> We think the problem is shyness. What works with her? Focusing on what she has written. (Soft pure)

It has been argued that 'difficulties in using criticism constructively lie at the heart of many students' problems in learning' (Rana 2000: 133). Feedback can be eagerly received if it is perceived to come from a well-intentioned source:

> In my first academic post I got friendly with an academic colleague. I was very unconfident about my writing for publication. He would correct grammar and English and would ask the awkward questions, even though he knew nothing about my field. (Hard applied)

Ethics and the relationship between academic and student

Several codes of practice can inform this relationship. The European Mentoring Council (EMC 2008), the British Psychological Society and the General Teaching Council (until 2012) all have elements which apply to this work.

The EMC code identifies the boundary issue. It explicitly says that the coach (academic) has to recognise the limits of their competence and refer the client to another specialist if they reach those limits. It also emphasises that the coach has responsibilities even once the relationship has finished – especially in connection with confidentiality and intellectual property.

The British Psychological Society has a code of conduct which highlights four principles: respect, competence, integrity and responsibility (BPS 2008).

In general it is better to not put yourself in a position where anyone can allege favouritism or incompetence on any level and involving another academic or co-supervisor can be a helpful way of averting such allegations.

Can you identify degenerate patterns in relationships?

There are at least four potential abuses of the supervisory relationship, they are similar to the problems highlighted in the previous chapter when we looked at toxic mentoring, but I want to be more explicit here so that the reader can interrogate their own practice.

The supervisor could be seeking *commercial gain* from the student's research, this could be direct financial reward for claiming a part in an invention that was not their due, or putting in funding bids excluding the student and overemphasising their role in the work so far carried out. The supervisor can be seeking *intellectual gain*, where they learn so much from the student, and seek to enhance their own reputation from claiming authorship where they have contributed little, or they can be so controlling that they will not let the student make their own mistakes. There are problems associated with seeking *sexual gain*, but the final problem area is much more difficult to put a satisfactory boundary around. *Friendship gain* can be legitimate, but where it is an abuse of power or feeding a need in the academic to be loved it can become oppressive for the student.

It is easy to talk about establishing boundaries, empathy without intimacy, or holding on to a detached concern without indulging in the emotional investment that gets people into trouble, but it is much more difficult to do. Sometimes external help from a counsellor needs to be sought, and if it is sought in time it can make all the difference to the experience for all parties concerned. There are ethical issues to be addressed about conflicts of interest where an academic is seeking gain and these are compounded when the academic has a role in assessment, in these difficult cases a discussion with the programme manager or director of postgraduate studies will be needed.

How do you end the academic and supervisory relationship?

There are elements of overlap between a primary mentoring relationship, and this approach to supervision, so the advice in ending an academic or supervisory relationship is the same: summarise the journey, celebrate and do something appropriately different. Before the relationship in this format ends, have a conversation about your expectations of what will happen afterwards.

Do you look forward to continued regular contact, occasional postcards or professionally working together, or are you celebrating the end of a difficult time for one or both of you, and a time that neither of you want to revisit very much?

There will be references to be written and these need to be professionally done in accordance with the prevailing advice from your institution. I always like to show my students the references I write for them, because I feel I should be able to be honest to them as well as about them and this helps to avoid any inaccuracies, but some academics find this inhibiting. Students in the UK will have the right to see what is written about them in references if they should appeal or seek to see them under the Freedom of Information Act.

The best relationships arise where values and expectations are shared, where trust is high, feedback is kindly but honest, where problems become opportunities to learn and all parties are respected for their contribution.

Box 7.6 summarises the main questions that academics need to ask themselves to ensure that they are clear about how they are going to maintain a healthy relationship.

Box 7.6 Self assessment questions to help manage the relationship

1   Can you like some aspect of each student you teach? Can you see some potential in them?
2   Are you aware of the boundaries that you are not prepared to cross?
3   Is the student aware of the boundaries that are not to be crossed?
4   How much time are you willing and realistically able to spend on non-academic (i.e. pastoral, career and social) matters? Are your students aware of this?
5   Are you clear about when it is appropriate to see students individually and when it is better to meet them as a group?
6   There are limits to the pastoral support you can provide, where else can your student get this support?
7   Have you decided what celebrations are going to take place when the student completes their studies with you?
8   When the academic relationship is due to be completed, can you acknowledge the positive aspects of the students you teach and the way you have worked together?

Further reading

Haynes, K., Metcalf, J., and Videlier, T. (2009) *What Do Researchers Do? First Destinations of Doctoral Graduates by Subject.* Cambridge: Careers Research and Advisory Centre (CRAC).

Macfarlane, B. (2004) *Teaching with Integrity: The Ethics of Higher Education Practice.* London: Routledge Falmer.

Murphy, N., Bain, J., and Conrad, L. (2007) 'Orientations to higher degree supervision. *Higher Education.* 53: 209–234.

Rogers, C. (1967) *On Becoming a Person: A Therapist's View of Psychotherapy.* London: Constable.

Rogers, C. (1983) *Freedom to Learn in the 80's.* Columbus, OH: Charles E. Merrill.

Chapter 8

Using the framework

Advantages and disadvantages of each approach

This need for combining approaches becomes more obvious when we examine the advantages and disadvantages of each approach. The supervisor will want to choose their approaches so that they combine the advantages, help the student to carry out the best possible research in a timely manner, be able to defend their thesis and for both parties to enjoy the process as much as possible. They will want to minimise risks of unnecessary delay, relationship breakdown or failure.

The advantages of following the functional approach are that the research project is managed according to the procedures of the institution, the student understands the stages that need to be processed, records are kept, and timetables are adhered to. However, the disadvantage is that learning and research are not always 'timetableable' activities. Original knowledge is not always waiting around the next corner to be discovered at the time of the student's choosing. A functional approach might fulfil the institution's needs, but it might not allow for the highest quality work or the most rewarding relationships.

An academic who is keen to enculturate their student, might create a rewarding and collaborative department, where the in-group has a strong identity. Conversely the disadvantage of this approach is that if the student wants to do their research differently, or even to behave slightly differently, the group might reject them.

Critical thinking is often thought to be the heart of supervision; its strength is that if it is appropriately carried out then sound arguments will ensue, but a slavish adherence to the altar of critical thinking can leave little room for creativity, and creativity is important if new and original thinking is to emerge. Critical thinking applied inhumanely can also be destructive, both of new ideas and of people.

The emancipatory approach encourages personal growth and an ability to cope with change. It is the cornerstone of much counselling and the tools of the mentor (see Chapter 6) are powerful and can be life-changing. However, that power equally has a dark side, for example, the academic who has not resolved issues over their own self-worth might be tempted to use their student to bolster a failing ego.

A warm and equal relationship, which continues after graduation, can be one of the most rewarding aspects of supervision; both parties gain in their self-esteem in this scenario. The darker aspect that also needs recognising is that in any relationship there is an opportunity for harassment (on either side) and if one person unexpectedly walks away from the relationship, the other can feel hurt and abandoned.

These advantages and disadvantages of the different approaches are summarised in Table 8.1.

The boundaries within the framework and their limitations

The following quotations illustrate how the boundaries are blurred in practice. In the next quotation the supervisor is talking about defining the limits of a research project and they are using elements of functional, critical thinking and relationship approaches to explain this.

> One of the most important things that I have to point out to new students as their advisor is that the research project does not have to be a magnum opus. It is only an advanced piece of work for assessment and it can always be improved upon. It is the start of a career, not its culmination. In the beginning I thought that it was vital to spend time building a good relationship with my students, I am not decrying that now, but I put more emphasis on setting clear targets, giving detailed feedback on their written work and encouraging them to publish as soon as they are nearly ready. (Soft pure)

In this extract, the supervisor is talking about how they are aiming to develop transferable or generic skills – this could be a functional activity, but here it is also described as an emancipatory activity.

> I've always viewed postgraduate study as part of a life skill system. In other words, I didn't view it as purely as a route to a qualification so I tried to equip all my postgraduate students with a skills set. Obviously the skills set you would expect from any advanced study but also, for example ... I usually asked them where they wanted to work. And for my PhD students I could usually find introduction for their next step in their career. (Hard applied)

This supervisor describes how they moved from working on critical thinking and it moved to become an exciting intellectual relationship.

Table 8.1 Advantages and disadvantages of different conceptual approaches to teaching and supervising research students

	Functional	Enculturation	Critical thinking	Emancipation	Relationship
ADVANTAGES	Clarity	Encourages standards, participation, identity, community formation	Rational inquiry, fallacy exposed	Personal growth, ability to cope with change	Lifelong working partnerships
	Consistency				Enhanced self-esteem
	Progress can be monitored				
DISADVANTAGES	Rigidity when confronted with the creation of original knowledge	Low tolerance of internal difference, sexist, ethnicised regulation (Cousin & Deepwell 2005)	Denial of creativity, can belittle or depersonalise student	Toxic mentoring (Darling 1985) where tutor abuses power	Potential for harassment, abandonment or rejection

I've had other students who have been an absolute delight to work with. I'll give you an example, I remember one student ... I'd come up with an idea for a, in a computer aided design technique which was literally a thousand times faster than the conventional techniques. But he brought elegancy to it which I personally found inspiring.

And we would literally spend hours working on a whiteboard thinking of the really elegant ways, and it was more like working with a research colleague. We were literally bouncing off each other on a day-to-day basis making what we felt were great strides. Together I found it as exciting as the student did. He was a slightly more mature student. (Hard applied)

The next quote illustrates the importance of starting with a functional approach and then enculturation:

I realised, for example, we did need to set objectives and we needed to assess against those whereas (before) we just used to write notes around meetings we'd have ...

I realised in terms of timing, (I got a) much better sense of when students needed to start writing papers. Many people don't even do that until they have finished their thesis and viva. But I realised that you could often encourage students towards the end of the second year to seriously consider putting papers in for conferences and writing journal papers. And actually that was extremely positive in terms of their development because they then became more motivated and changed their view because of that. And it took me a little while to realise that. I think I've left far too many of them well into the third year before we were writing papers earlier on in my career.

I think that the advice I was offering became much more focused, which was of more use to the students too. So I could see exactly what they needed to be doing, when they were doing it, and how to solve what they perceived as a blockage to their thinking.

So, in other words, (formulating) what I'd done by simply working with them or (being very) energetic at the beginning. (Hard applied)

Another supervisor talked about the need to have a functional approach, but to blend it with critical thinking:

I think you have to be willing to give the time to it. I think it is extremely important. You have to be willing to study the problem they are looking at so you can offer good advice and make sure you are right too. It's not only, it's not only, it's essential to do it but it is also interesting.

You have to be interested in their problem ... it does worry me at times that people take PhD students on simply to achieve the matrix of having numbers when the motivation isn't there to do it. I can honestly say I never did that. In fact if I had a lot of PhD students I would stop doing other things to make sure I could provide the supervision. And, for example, I always set up a pattern of supervision meetings so that we knew where we were all going. We would indeed be meeting every week. How often we met varied. In a new PhD student I'd probably be meeting them three times to week to get them going, if they were the typical student. If they needed a bit more support, I might meet them every day, as I mentioned earlier. Usually, towards the end of the second year when things were cruising, they probably would have been happier meeting for an hour to two per week. In fact usually at that time ... they'd say, well look we really don't need to meet so often. I'd say, I think we should, let's get together. And then sometimes during the thesis formation we would meet more, you know, it varied, as you can imagine. (Hard applied)

The next academic talked about the boundary between enculturation and the relationship, and how they felt a special sense of responsibility particularly for overseas students – this was a theme that emerged in several interviews but not all academics are in a position to be able to offer this type of help:

I've obviously had cases where, overseas students in particular, have had extreme poverty, I've managed, through research funding or money I've brought in through consultancy, to help them. And I do think you have an obligation to, and that's part of the PhDs, I think there is a special relationship between supervisors and students in a sense that you build a bond which is beyond the technical and academic elements of it. And I think the net result is very positive, it's professional, I'm not suggesting it is about being your best friend or something, but I do feel as a supervisor you have responsibilities to be concerned about the welfare and pastoral wellbeing of the student beyond their studies. I think you have to draw a very careful line. (Hard applied)

It is in combining different approaches to solving a problem that we begin to see the real strength of this framework. The problems presented in the tables in this chapter are an amalgamation of typical problems and solutions suggested by groups of academics attending workshops and seminars. The suggested solutions are simple versions of a much longer discussion but the contents can be adapted to reflect the norms in your institution and extended to be used as mini-case studies. In looking at the summary table of some suggested answers, it quickly becomes apparent that none of the approaches are either all right or all wrong. They are designed to stimulate thought and are not presented as being definitive. The problems presented assume that students are working in small study groups or one-to-one tutorials; most of the scenarios can be adjusted to meet the needs of different students and larger groups.

The following case study is an example of the extended discussion that might follow the presentation of a case study to a group of research supervisors. These types of cases are intended to trigger discussion and to enable academics to share their own successes, fears and other experiences.

Using the framework to help to respond to failure

Your doctoral student has just failed their transfer. The feedback was that the student's proposed study would contribute nothing original, that this ground has already been well covered by previous researchers. The student is distraught and says they have never failed any university exam before.

If the supervisor uses the functional approach inappropriately at this time (for example suggesting: 'shall we agree a deadline of one month for you to rewrite the transfer document?') to a distressed student who does not know where to turn, that student may withdraw at this point. An alternative might be an enculturation approach (for example suggesting: 'shall we meet again in a month, and in the interim I suggest you compare your work with these two successful transfer reports?'). The critical thinking approach might include a suggestion that the student looks at how many different angles this study could be approached from – to find a new audience or perception. Whether or not this suggestion is a helpful spur or a push too far at this stage would depend on the student, but it would be possible to gain a reaction from the student and adjust the approach accordingly. An emancipatory approach could include support and challenge ('don't worry, this has happened before and in the end the student I am thinking of graduated without any problems, you will need to learn how to handle critical feedback and make it work for you') and a relationship approach might include some appropriate self-disclosure such as: 'I remember being devastated when I got my first referee's report back condemning a journal article I had put so much work into, perhaps you feel like that too at the moment?'

It is impossible to prescribe approaches, or a blend of approaches out of context, but it is possible for the research supervisor to ask sufficient questions to determine what combination of approaches is most likely to be successful. Questions such as 'have you ever had feedback like this before?', 'how does this make you feel about the timetable we had agreed?', 'what can I most usefully do to help you at the moment?' will all give useful clues. There are some key issues that the research supervisor is going to need to make judgements about: establishing the roots of the problem – was this just a rather hasty piece of work or is there a problem with intellectual ability; are there approaches which will help the student to become more creative (see Chapter 1); how can you help the student to understand more about what has already been covered; how do you help the student to identify that learning from failure enables resilience, and that this is a key characteristic of an effective researcher? If you advised the student that the work would be acceptable you may have to restore the student's confidence in you as an adviser; and when faced with any very difficult dilemma it is always wise to ask who else might be able to help in this situation.

Using the framework to help the student conceptualise at the right level

A common problem for supervisors, particularly in the early stages of a research project, is how to help the student who is not thinking at the right level. We worry about a student who seems to be reading the right literature, but is only describing, not summarising it, not critically analysing, conceptualising, and theorising what they are reading. We can use the framework to deconstruct different approaches to this problem.

Functional

The academic working from this approach might take it in stages: they would spend some time enabling the student to understand what 'conceptualisation' means. They could give the student examples of themes and show them how to find the underlying concepts, and then give them a series of exercises where they have to do it for themselves. The final stage is to give students articles or research findings and ask them to conceptualise them.

They might also check whether or not the student has been to any academic writing tutorials that the university provides.

Enculturation

Here the academic would give the student examples of good practice within the discipline. They might ask the student to analyse a seminal article and describe why it is good, or get them to read several literature reviews and identify what was good or bad about each one.

Critical thinking

The academic would need to discuss in some detail what conceptualisation is and why (or whether) it is important. As in 'enculturation' the academic might make them critique good and bad examples of conceptualisation, but then they would ask them to review and critique their own work in the same way.

Emancipation

Here the debate could be more about the advantages and limits of conceptualisation, and whether there are other ways to synthesise past knowledge and prepare for an uncertain future. The academic would be keen to encourage out-of-the-box thinking and might, for example, give them an (impossible) hypothesis to conceptualise.

Relationship

The academic would need to check their own ability to describe the level and type of work they require, they would ask themselves 'have I made it clear what I am looking for?' They would want to understand what the student thought conceptualisation is. They may need to look for cultural barriers to this type of synthesis and criticism and ask themselves if they need to give the student permission to critique experts' work.

These approaches are summarised in Table 8.2, and from this it is possible to see how a combination of approaches will probably be the strongest option.

The student might react negatively to any single form of approach – for example using only the functional approach might be felt by the student to be excessively programmed and reductionist. Use only the relationship approach and the student might enjoy supervision meetings, but not be fully aware of the progress (or the implications of not making that progress) that he or she is expected to make between meetings. Using the critical thinking approach on its own could leave the student with outstanding analytical and problem-solving skills but a lack of awareness of how this might help their own journey and career. It is a sensitive and timely combination of approaches that will lead to the most successful outcomes for the research student.

Helping students towards independence

All the academics who were interviewed said that one measure of success that they used to assess progress was how independent their student became. On further analysis, dependence and independence meant slightly different things within each approach. So, for example, if an academic was working from an approach where they want their student to become a full member of the discipline, they would expect the student to move from needing to be shown what to do, to a position where the student knew exactly what a member of that discipline would do next, and could do it.

However, if the academic was working from an emancipatory approach, their first concern would be to support the student's perception of self-efficacy and self worth, and when the student had become independent, they would be able to evaluate for themselves whether any disciplines had anything to

Table 8.2 Illustration of different approaches to working with a student who cannot conceptualise at the right level

	Functional	Enculturation	Critical thinking	Emancipation	Relationship development
The student who cannot conceptualise or theorise at the right level	Explain what conceptualisation means. Give short exercises to build skills	Give examples of how others in the discipline have done it well	Explore conceptualisation and why it is important	Explore ways of synthesising knowledge and preparing for the future	Are there cultural barriers? Are the requirements clear?

offer their next path, know what their goals were, what they wanted to do and be able to do it.

The importance of a more equal power relationship (it can never be completely equal whilst the academic holds the key to the upgrading and assessment process) becomes apparent when we look at independence in the relationship development approach. Here the dependent student will be seeking approval, but when they become more independent the student and academic will both be able to negotiate conflict and boundaries with relative ease and both will feel equally capable of withdrawing from the relationship if they need to (see Table 8.3).

Using the framework to support student(s) through various stages

In the interviews with experienced research supervisors it became clear that they planned well ahead when thinking about the students that they wanted to work with intensively. Some encouraged students in their lectures to think about further research even as they began an undergraduate career, others involved their students in their own research by recruiting undergraduates to undertake holiday work such as checking references. Recruiting students who are likely to be able to complete, who will work well with your existing team and who are able to do the work at the right level is obviously going to make supervising them much easier. It is not always possible for new academics to be quite so selective – they may well be asked to take over students working in an area where they feel their expertise is patchy – so the sooner the academic can become proactive in this field the better. It is possible to use the framework to explore the different approaches to recruitment, and to create a meld of approaches that is most likely to result in a successful outcome for all concerned. The functional approach will be to have a clear timetable for recruitment, to advertise appropriately and in good time, to list the competencies required then to interview against this list. Human Resource Departments will be familiar with this procedure and able to provide substantial guidance. The weakness of the competencies approach is that it measures past performance and is not quite so good at identifying potential where there is no substantial evidence of experience. To bridge this gap the academic may need to move into 'critical thinking mode' and use hypothetical questions to try to ascertain creativity and flexibility. When recruiting full-time research students, the academic will probably want to incorporate them into an existing team, offering some work experience and involving the team in the recruitment procedure. The academic who takes the humanistic approach will welcome signs of initiative and interest from enquiring students and will be looking to see how this research project might help the student reframe their identity. Finally, and often unacknowledged, is the 'gut reaction' that we have when we first meet people. Examining

Table 8.3 Concepts of teaching and supervision compared with dependence and independence

	PROFESSIONAL ROLE			PERSONAL SELF		
	Functional	*Enculturation*	*Critical thinking*	*Emancipation*	*Relationship development*
DEPENDENCE	Student needs explanation of stages to be followed and direction through them	Student needs to be shown what to do	Student learns the questions to ask, the frameworks to apply	Student seeks affirmation of self-worth	Student seeks approval
INDEPENDENCE	Student can programme own work, follow own timetables competently	Student can follow discipline's epistemological demands independently	Student can critique own work	Student autonomous. Can decide how to be, where to go, what to do, where to find information	Student demonstrates appropriate reciprocity and has power to withdraw

that gut reaction a little more carefully is wise because it can be based on superficial judgements that should not be guiding our selection criteria and that may not stand the test of time. Table 8.4 summarises how the framework can be used to help the academic think through the recruitment process that they want to adopt.

In terms of significance and setting the tone for the future relationship, the first meeting creates first impressions and can have a powerful impact on subsequent progress. It is not so much the details of what is discussed that will have the lingering resonance, the student will probably be quite overwhelmed and those details will need some repetition later, the test of a successful first meeting is that by the end of it does the student feel clear about the timetable, that there are other people in the department they can also talk to, that there is some clarity around how 'original knowledge' will be assessed, that their study will be personally life-enhancing and that they are welcome? Table 8.5 summarises some of the tools that the academic can use to ensure that the first meeting is as helpful as possible.

Sometimes the academic faces a situation where, for whatever reason, they become frustrated because the student does not comply with requests, protocols or procedures. Where this applies to experiments it might constitute a health and safety risk, then an emergency procedure will need to be instituted. If it constitutes an ethical risk the academic will need to consult other members of staff, perhaps a director of studies or chair of a relevant ethics committee.

Of course there are many possible reasons for this type of problem emerging: the student may think that they are claiming their right to academic freedom or they may not have understood the instructions and be unwilling to expose their ignorance. Exploring the cause of the problem is central to establishing which approach(es) are likely to result in a successful outcome.

Where there are serious breaches that could become disciplinary offences, the academic may be wise to plan to meet with the student and with the co-supervisor or another academic. Entering into a phase of issuing warnings requires detailed planning and documentation, and this must be done hand in hand with the offer of substantial training and guidance. Table 8.6 has a summary of some of the approaches that the academic may want to consider.

Students working on research at a distance present particular issues to academics; it means that the academic will have to take extra trouble to get to know them on-line and over skype or other voice-activated media; the framework can be applied to teaching on-line as well as face to face and interactions can fall into each of (or a combination of) approaches.

Where the student comes from a different culture, this can offer an opportunity for the academic to learn about it and it may offer new ways of doing research. In the case illustrated in Table 8.7, a couple of issues have become conflated, the student is obviously adept at manipulating the data but interpreting it is harder, they are finding it difficult to construct a written

Table 8.4 Approaches to recruiting research students

Functional	Enculturation	Critical thinking	Emancipation	Relationship development
• Well-organised recruitment procedure, clear timetable planned well in advance. Specific competencies and experience required clearly identified. • Emphasis on looking for a track record of work production on time. • Funding for fees and living expenses ascertained. • The necessary University resources identified in advance.	• Take account of references and recommendations. • Create opportunities before confirming appointment to see if they will fit in with the team. • Identify and encourage previous students to apply.	• Listen to the types of questions they ask. • Are they able to challenge the things you say? • Explore their history of anticipating or resolving problems. • Use exam results as a bar.	• Let them find you, the student needs to be actively seeking. • Make sure that minority groups are aware of the opportunities available.	• Look for enthusiasm, honesty and trustworthiness. • Use social events as part of the recruitment campaign. • Compare values – can we work together?

Ensure you follow your institution's best practice when recruiting students.

Table 8.5 Planning the first meeting

Functional	Enculturation	Critical thinking	Emancipation	Relationship development
• Go through codes of practice. • Agree a timetable for future meetings. • Create a project plan with milestones and ensure they are written in supervisor's and student's diaries. • Clarify the roles of primary and co-supervisors and advisors. • Explain the 'rules of engagement'. • Discuss an outline publication policy. • Talk about what forms will need to be completed when.	• Introduce the student to the team. • Invite student to team meetings/ seminars. • Introduce student to key authors/ texts. • Set tasks where the student will learn 'how we do it here'. • Explain what the team has done so far and agree what the student is going to start with.	• Ascertain subject knowledge and identify any gaps. • Encourage the student to begin to identify/create their own 'critical toolkit'. • Share expectations. • Warn about the tricky questions. • Get the student to prepare some tricky questions.	• Encourage the student to present their own plans. • Explore their inner motivation for wanting to do this research. • Encourage the student to identify outsiders who might provide support/ illumination. • Ask the student what they want to achieve from the process.	• Discuss the relationship, how it might go. • Discuss what the student can do if they are unhappy at any point. • Establish mutual expectations. • Invite them to tea/ coffee breaks with other members of the team. • Prepare them for the process – the hard road ahead and the good bits.

Table 8.6 Approaches to managing the student who does not carry out the experiments as you have repeatedly asked them to do

Functional	Enculturation	Critical thinking	Emancipation	Relationship development
• Create a clear timetable. • List step by step, in writing and orally, what is to be done and get the student to repeat it back to you in their own words. • Restate deadlines. • Issue warnings (informal or formal as appropriate). • Offer retraining.	• Have a group/team meeting to discuss together how to proceed with these experiments in general. • Allocate a mentor to this student from the group.	• Give ultimatums. • Analyse possible reasons for the lack of compliance (e.g. cultural differences, misunderstanding, lack of agreement about priorities). • Explore with the student what the eventual outcome will be if this continues.	• Ask the student how they think things are going. • Get the student to self-assess their performance and to compare their performance with others.	• Discuss why they do not work in the way you have asked. • Explain the problems that it gives you.

argument. That issue can arise for any student doing research, but in this case there are distance learning and cross-cultural issues implied as well.

Students doing research are not immune to plagiarism, but the nature of the work they are doing and the closer amount of supervision that they get normally makes it less of a problem. However it does still occur and we need to be alert to good practice. The most difficult cases that arise are those where work is 'ghost written' for the student, the commonest problem is with the 'copy and paste' type of plagiarism, frequently taken from work that already exists on the internet.

If you are concerned about this issue, a good text to refer to is Carroll (2002) *A Handbook for Deterring Plagiarism in Higher Education*. Carroll objectively explores how to prevent, detect and punish plagiarism. 'Designing out plagiarism' is another useful handout that is available from the University of Surrey website at http://www.surrey.ac.uk/cead/resources/documents/Designing_out_plagiarism.pdf. Table 8.8 illustrates how a range of approaches can be taken to minimise the risks of students becoming involved in plagiarism.

Some students present as more chaotic than others, and of course some students are faced with very chaotic lives. Where students are continuously late, the issue in research supervision is more one of a potential clash of expectations. Some academics are not known for their time-keeping either! So the first question is to ascertain how important timeliness is to this particular piece of work. In many cases it is also an issue of courtesy, and poor time-keeping in one part of life might indicate a potential employability issue in the future. When lateness is combined with the bare minimum of work, it does become a very difficult problem because there is always little time to help the student to improve. Table 8.9 has a range of suggestions for approaching this tricky combination of issues.

Students may be doing research individually, isolated in their Humboltian towers, but it is more likely that they will be working in small teams – and it is often more productive when they are.

Where research is being carried out as part of the undergraduate curriculum, inevitably there will be a larger group working together, but it is also possible now that we have many graduate schools, for academics to be supervising large groups of doctoral students. There is evidence that increasing class size has a detrimental effect on quality, there is also concern about the use of doctoral or post-doctoral students to do some teaching, particularly when students in the UK are facing increasing fees and likely to demand world-class teachers (Gibbs 2010). This means that the academic will have to develop some exceptional management skills, their main responsibility becomes to create the environment that will enable students to flourish, rather than to supervise each one individually.

One argument for using doctoral students, post-doctoral students or adjunct professors to do some teaching, is that we have to develop teaching

Table 8.7 How to manage the student who is good at presenting data but finds it difficult to construct the argument

Functional	Enculturation	Critical thinking	Emancipation	Relationship development
• Break the task down into smaller chunks. • Use leading questions to encourage a particular train of thought. • Reward early achievements. • Enable participation in programmes that teach 'English writing for academic purposes'.	• Use patch writing so that the student has to 'complete the gaps'. • Show the student good examples of work and discuss why they are good. • Get some post-doctoral students who might be familiar with this student's background to do some supervision. • Link to other students from the same country. • Get the student to discuss the implications of their work with fellow students.	• Make the critical frameworks explicit. • Discuss the normal procedures in their culture and get the student to explore these further. • Give the student good and bad quality examples of work and ask them to analyse them and describe the difference.	• Name the problem (like a diagnosis, naming a problem can help the student to understand it and take responsibility for managing it). • Get them to evaluate their own performance. • If they fail at any of the milestones, pre-warn them of this possibility and be prepared to identify some learning from the experience.	• Find other students or colleagues from that culture to try to understand more about this student's pedagogical expectations. • Be honest about the difficulties you are experiencing as a supervisor and clear about what you want the student to do. • Meet the student face to face – either finding a way of bringing them to you, or you to them. • Find a colleague in the same country who can have a meeting with the student.

Table 8.8 How to handle the student you suspect of plagiarism

Functional	Enculturation	Critical thinking	Emancipation	Relationship development
• Ensure the guidelines are clear and that all students have undertaken some training on referencing, avoiding collusion and acceptable paraphrasing. • Ask for drafts to give feedback on. • Document concerns carefully. • Discuss issues with plagiarism officers/ Dean of Students.	• Talk to the whole team about research ethics, discuss examples from elsewhere, where there have been difficulties. • Talk to the whole team about the culture and importance of the department's reputation. • Arrange a seminar for the whole group on plagiarism and academic practice. • Explore possible cultural pedagogical differences. • Get students to give feedback on each other's draft outlines before they start writing.	• Review the tasks you are setting. Are they encouraging plagiarism. • Get students to analyse their own work on plagiarism detection software. • Set students presentations to give and critique so they have to respond to questions from peers as well as academics.	• Explore the student's ambitions and how plagiarism might affect them. • Explore hypothetically the potential outcome of plagiarism if it were replicated on a wider scale. • Talk about ethical values.	• Explain that you feel personally very disappointed. • Discuss what happens when trust is broken. • Ask what else you could do to help.

Table 8.9 Approaches to managing the student who is always late to meetings and does the bare minimum of work

Functional	Enculturation	Critical thinking	Emancipation	Relationship development
• Go back to the original agreements and compare them with reality. • Ensure that you have full agreement to the time set for the next meeting. • Document violations. • Identify consequences. • Give warnings. • Remind the student of downgrading possibilities.	• Explain that membership of the group is at risk. • Remind the whole group of the standards you required. • Identify what is at risk e.g. exchanges, conferences, meetings etc.	• Reassess the student's intellectual capacity – are they brilliant but uninterested? • Assess the risk to the overall project – how important is this?	• Are you late yourself? What quality of feedback do you give? Assess the culture you have established. • Link their current behaviour to past behaviour (is there a pattern?) and explore the student's future objectives – how will success now help them in the future?	• Have a conversation, tell them you are disappointed, say what potential you see in them, try to ascertain what the real problem is.

skills in the next generation and they have to start somewhere, another is that they frequently put a great deal of energy into preparing their sessions and a third argument is that they may be closer in years to the majority of students and therefore able to access popular examples and rhetoric more easily when explaining complex principles. What we do need to do is to ensure that they have sound subject knowledge and have sufficiently developed their pedagogical approaches and personality. Training post-doctoral or doctoral students to teach and manage students doing research is one of the ways of managing large groups. Table 8.10 looks at a range of approaches.

From time to time we meet very capable students, sometimes outstanding, and yet a combination of personal circumstances, personality and sometimes the nature of the research combine to emotionally and physically exhaust the student. This can worry or even frighten the academic, and the student might be resistant to help because they are desperately worried about what will happen if they demonstrate any fragility. The framework can be used to create a range of approaches to dealing with this situation – which in any case is one that needs to be handled with extreme caution. Table 8.11 illustrates some of these approaches.

As we have seen in Chapter 3, assessment of research takes many forms even at the doctoral level. In Sweden the public defence is more of a ritual because peer-reviewed publication is essential before a thesis can go forward for examination. In Australia the external examiners will compile detailed written reports because travelling across time zones is problematic. In the UK a viva will be conducted face to face with two or three examiners interviewing the student sometimes over several hours. At masters and undergraduate level there still may be assessment of a written dissertation and it is important at all levels that students are prepared for the types of assessment criteria that will be applied.

Trafford and Leshem (2008) argue that the hidden should be made visible, and students should be prepared for assessment from the very beginning. Jackson and Tinkler (2007) and Tinkler and Jackson (2004) have written two well-regarded texts for examiners. In Chapter 3 we looked at assessment as part of the functional approach to managing research, however we can use the whole framework to look at how to prepare a student for their assessment and Table 8.12 illustrates this.

Matching student and supervisor

A key and complex question is whether or not the academic and student match. The matching process is not easy to define, and is best explored in terms of looking at subject expertise, supervision expertise, the time both have available and expectations. The expectations of the supervisor need to be made explicit, revealed at appropriate times and often repeated so that the student hears them and applies them to different parts of the student process.

Table 8.10 How to manage a large group of students doing research

Functional	Enculturation	Critical thinking	Emancipation	Relationship development
• Ensure that all supervisors/ academics know of the procedures that you want followed. • Arrange training sessions for co-supervisors. • Delegate to post-doctoral students and arrange appropriate training for them. • Clearly allocate roles and responsibilities. • Ensure research supervision has its rewards and recognition. • Ensure that your answers to questions posed by individual or small groups of students are available to all the other students – maybe using web-based technologies.	• Emphasise the team and the need to back each other up and work together. • Use web-based activities to communicate. • Organise regular lunch-time seminars/journal clubs and attend them yourself.	• Analyse what structures/ processes will work in reviewing each other's papers. • Identify strengths and weaknesses of members of your team. • Consider using web technology to encourage group critiquing skills e.g. by posting a journal article for all students to comment on.	• Develop facilitation skills amongst the members of your team so that they can mentor and support each other. • Provide links to a wide range of interesting resources and encourage further individual study.	• Ensure that social events are organised, and attend them. • Consider including partners and families. • Organise team-building events.

Table 8.11 How to handle the student you think is facing burn-out

Functional	Enculturation	Critical thinking	Emancipation	Relationship development
• Find expert help for the student. • Renegotiate the individual's study plan. • Change some deadlines to take the pressure off.	• If appropriate, involve the whole group. • Look for ways of getting other group members to support this individual and their work.	• Define burnout. • Analyse the reasons for burnout. Has it happened in your team before? Is there a pattern? • Think of a number of ways of keeping the project on track.	• Ask whether the student wants to talk or to be left alone. • Be prepared to move into a counselling role. • Try to understand how the student sees the situation, what is behind this stress and support them, find out if they need other help.	• Show sympathy. • Make time to talk. • Take some of the work off the student's shoulders for a while. • Arrange other events to take the student's mind off work.

Table 8.12 How to prepare the students for their assessment

Functional	Enculturation	Critical thinking	Emancipation	Relationship development
• Ensure that the assessment criteria are clear. • Ensure that the timetable is clear. • Give all the assessors all the information they need. • Enable formative assessment and feedback for the student in good time.	• Encourage students to pre-assess each other's work against the assessment criteria. • Get previous students to talk about their experience of the assessment process. • Rehearse the process with a group of students.	• Explore the implications of the assessment criteria early on. • Get the students to identify the questions they might be asked. • Rehearse the process and reflect on it afterwards.	• Involve the students in the design of appropriate assessment criteria. • Help the students to pre-assess their own work and identify how secure they felt about each judgement. • Help the student to learn from any failure. • Rehearse the process.	• Ensure that no student could believe that a personal relationship with any other student might prejudice the assessor's judgement. • Ensure that students feel that you recognise the amount of work they have put in, as well as affirming success and helping them to learn from any difficulties.

An example of this virtue of repetition came through one of the focus groups. One student said:

> Every time I pick up a journal article now I hear my supervisor saying to me 'what is wrong with this article – where are its weaknesses?' (Student, Psychology)

This is obviously an example of the critical thinking approach, but the smiling manner with which the student reported this suggested that the development of critical thinking had taken place within the context of a strong relationship.

Some supervisors feel that the matching process has been put under pressure by institutional requirements to take more students, as the following quotation from an experienced research supervisor illustrates:

> My first academic post was in 1972. There was a time when the relationship was more like a master/apprenticeship relationship. Now there is a lot of pressure that was not there before. Being pressurised to take people who are marginal to your own interests. Then you end up not being very authentic. So now there are a lot of subtle ways in which we end up with students who are not prepared, but we take them on and then leave them to their own devices. Then a dissatisfaction sets in that you are muddling through. Previously they really chose you and you would not hesitate to say no if you felt you could not get on. So if you end up with two people who are not really choosing each other … (Soft pure)

As Kiley identified (2006) key issues in identifying student expectations have been explored in literature from psychology, education and management fields.

Expectancy value theory suggests that students will be motivated to engage if they expect an outcome which they value, and research into self efficacy suggested that students will be motivated to engage if they anticipate success (Biggs & Moore 1993). The management literature suggests exploring four different sources of the expectations that students bring with them:

1 Word of mouth from previous students
2 Personal needs
3 Past experience (school or university)
4 Contacts from marketing department and university.

(Zeithaml, Parasuraman & Berry 1990)

Managing research is a process where the boundaries are inevitably less clear than in taught courses, so the literature suggests that the supervisor needs to answer the following key questions for each student at the outset:

1 Why you (the student) will find this useful
2 How you will succeed at it
3 What it is I want you to learn.

Over time we can use the framework to explore the students' needs at an even deeper level. We need to keep asking what the research student is seeking from the supervisor, and make it plain what we are able to offer (see Table 8.13). A discussion of this table between student and academic can be very fruitful.

The supervisor too has needs; they may want a significant part of their own research project to be carried out by a responsible, ethical and intelligent student; they may be isolated in that they are the expert in their field and want companions who are equally passionate about their research; they may have whole areas of their discipline that they have not been able to explore that they want uncovered. Revealing some of these motivations at appropriate times can help the student to feel an important part of the team or department and make the relationship more rewarding.

Table 8.14 condenses and summarises some of the different approaches to solving a further range of problems that have emerged in discussions with hundreds of supervisors, and is useful for quick reference, but it is when these approaches are elaborated upon and combined that they become really powerful.

All these solutions can look 'neat' when packaged in a paragraph in a book, and they will not apply directly to any of your students. However, if the academic who is faced with an apparently intractable problem thinks to themself 'in how many ways could I approach this?' the work of this chapter will be done and the chances of a successful outcome for everyone will be greater.

This framework has been shown as a matrix for the purposes of deconstruction and analysis, a more realistic map of the doctoral process is now given where you can see that functionality is all-surrounding. A student–academic relationship cannot exist outside an institutional context, but the red centre is redolent of the heart that this framework carefully puts back at the centre. Emancipation and enculturation are seen more in opposition and are connected by the other three approaches.

The framework is shown as a matrix throughout the rest of this book, but this is for ease of analysis, in practice the boundaries are fuzzy and it is perhaps better represented as a Venn diagram (Figure 8.1). The overarching frame is the functional approach; even though I have warned against overemphasising the functional approach, I recognise that without an organisational framework no accredited qualifications can be awarded.

Table 8.13 Identifying the students' motivation, objectives and needs

	Functional	Enculturation	Critical thinking	Emancipation	Relationship development
What students might be seeking	Certainty Clear Signposts Evidence of progress	Belonging Direction Career opportunities Role models	Ability to think in new ways Ability to recognise flaws in arguments	Self awareness Autonomy Self actualisation	Friendship Nurturing Equality

Table 8.14 Summary of different approaches to solving a range of problems

	Functional	Enculturation	Critical thinking	Emancipation	Relationship development
The student who is too dependent on the academic	Time limit meetings, stick to a prepared agenda, set goals.	Encourage student to seek answers elsewhere first e.g. peers and post-doctoral students.	Analyse the stages that a student goes through in order to become independent.	Explore how student has become independent in other aspects of life.	Discuss and set boundaries until a relationship of equals becomes possible.
The mature, experienced student that the new academic may find daunting	Be clear about your expertise as an academic.	Convey a sense of a whole new world opening up.	Explore different beliefs about knowledge.	Explore different research methods and methodologies.	Value and share student's experience and add to their understanding.
The student who is not producing any written work	Break the tasks down into smaller, shorter ones.	Can the peer group or post-doctoral students help?	Assess what has been produced and get student to extend it.	Are there other pressures?	Is the student finding the academic too critical?
The student who does not seem interested in their work any more	Increase regular meetings, follow-up absences.	Encourage attendance at conferences etc to make them feel part of the wider community.	Encourage them to present own work or critique others.	Find out what does motivate the student at the moment.	Share own passion for the subject and inspire the student.
Language and cultural differences	Ensure instructions are given orally and in writing, reinforce explanations.	Encourage participation in international and faith networks.	Only challenge when student is more confident.	Ask student to compare and contrast old and new environments.	Be supportive, help the student to feel safe.

The student who				
The student who wants to undertake risky fieldwork	Take legal advice on the university's responsibilities. Keep records of all advice given to the student.	Find examples of others who have worked in this area to discuss.	Undertake a detailed risk analysis.	Explore how the student feels about the worst and best possible outcomes.	Share personal concerns for their safety/efficacy.
The student who is working too quickly	Set longer deadlines, encourage wider reading; get student to make detailed notes.	Get student to convene a research group.	Ask student to critique own work.	Ask student what they want to get out of the postgraduate process – explore motivation.	Share learning experiences where deep learning has really happened.
The overconfident student	Set objectives: specific, measurable, achievable, relevant and time-defined (SMART).	Encourage student to participate in departmental seminars/journal clubs and get feedback from others.	Get the student to argue counter-views.	Let the student fail and support subsequent learning.	Establish own credibility as an academic.
The student who upsets the department	Ask the student to change their behaviour.	Explore with the student, how the department works and why.	Explore what causes problems in working relationships.	Ask the student how they want to be seen/regarded.	Describe the history of the culture in the department and jointly agree an action plan.
The student who wants careers advice	Recommend the careers office, careers fairs and web sites.	Identify vacancies in the discipline.	Ask students to chart others' career paths.	Explore the student's motivation and criteria.	Disclose own career path.

How do I know what kind of supervisor I am?

Bearing in mind the limitations of this framework, some people still find a self assessment tool useful for understanding the different approaches. Table 8.15a contains a questionnaire which encourages academics to think about their priorities in the supervisory process. To complete it, tick the box which most indicates how important each issue is to you, and then score it as indicated in Table 8.15b.

Understanding your score

This brief questionnaire is designed to help you look at your priorities and understand a little more about each of the conceptual approaches. It is not (yet) a validated instrument.

A common pattern is for academics and supervisors initially to feel competent in or to seek competence in one or two of the approaches. They may be unable to function effectively in other approaches until they feel they have mastered the functional approach then they extend their interests into discovering the effects using some of the other approaches with their students. If there is another pattern, it might be for academics to move from enculturation to emancipation over time. It may be that mastery of enculturation (the academic is confident in their ability to successfully induct their research student into the disciplinary way of thinking) frees the academic to feel confident in then setting the student free to explore their potential (emancipation).

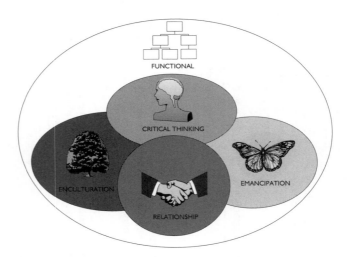

Figure 8.1 A map of the framework demonstrating interrelationships

Table 8.15a Academic's version – a questionnaire to enable greater understanding of the framework of approaches to research supervision (adapted from Lee 2008b)

Place a tick in one box on each line to indicate the level of importance you attach to that item	Unimportant … Important				
	1	2	3	4	5
1. I always allocate time well ahead for preparation, teaching and marking work for my postgraduate students.					
2. My postgraduate students learn quickly to embody the ethical principles and practices of this discipline.					
3. I want my postgraduate students to think critically, always to recognise flaws in articles, arguments or work that they see.					
4. It is important that my postgraduate students question themselves and understand why they are doing this research.					
5. My postgraduate students can manage their own and others' emotions appropriately.					
6. I consciously plan my teaching and supervision sessions so that my students will reach the appropriate level.					
7. I feel disappointed if good postgraduate students do not want to continue studying or working in the discipline.					
8. I want my postgraduate students to demonstrate an independence of mind.					
9. My postgraduate students are frequently transformed personally by the work they are doing.					
10. I enjoy being with my postgraduate students.					
11. A research student has to send me something they have written, to demonstrate they are making progress, before I will meet with them.					
12. It is important that my students understand the work of key researchers in my field.					
13. It is important to me that students can put forward counter-arguments.					
14. My students often go through a 'dark night of the soul' whilst doing their research, but emerge stronger for it.					
15. It is important that my students maintain positive working relationships with colleagues and help them as required.					
16. I note in my diary key dates for tutorials, annual reports etc, so I can monitor progress.					
17. I frequently show examples of interesting and excellent work in my field to my postgraduate students.					
18. Successful postgraduate students are able to validate or evaluate their arguments in a broad or interdisciplinary way.					
19. My postgraduate students learn to reframe the important questions.					
20. My postgraduate students enthuse others with their interest in their work.					

Table 8.15b Score sheet – add the scores up and it will give you some idea of your priorities as a supervisor

Q no	Score	Q no	Score	Q No	Score	Q no	Score	Q no	Score
1		2		3		4		5	
6		7		8		9		10	
11		12		13		14		15	
16		17		18		19		20	
Total function score		Total enculturation score		Total critical thinking score		Total emancipation score		Total relationships score	

How do I know what approaches my student will find most helpful?

There is another version of this questionnaire (Table 8.16a and b) that you can give to your students, and comparing your profile with theirs can lead to them understanding more clearly why you might respond or create certain situations to encourage their learning.

Understanding your score

This brief questionnaire is designed to help students look at priorities and understand a little more about each of the conceptual approaches to research. It is not (yet) a validated instrument.

A common pattern is for students who are achievement oriented, initially to be driven by external deadlines, e.g. for transfer or annual reports (a functional approach). As time moves on they may extend their interests into discovering more about how things are done successfully in their field or discipline (enculturation). The research process requires developing skills in intellectual rigour and analysis, and for some students developing these thinking skills is the most important aspect of their work (critical thinking). Students who see the research process as a journey of self-discovery as well as intellectual growth and enquiry may find that their intrinsic motivation propels them along new paths and into unforeseen careers (emancipation). For some students and supervisors, the most important element is that they are in a professional relationship where there is integrity and trust (relationships).

Students can use this questionnaire to compare their answers with those of their supervisors and fellow students, to understand why their supervisor might be acting in a certain way and to articulate more clearly what type of support they might find helpful.

Table 8.16a Student's version – a questionnaire to enable greater understanding of the framework of approaches to research as a student (adapted from Lee 2008b)

Place a tick in one box on each line to indicate the level of importance you attach to that item	Unimportant … Important				
	1	2	3	4	5
1. I always like to have a date arranged for the next meeting before I leave the current session.					
2. I want to understand and be able to replicate the ethical principles and practices of this discipline.					
3. It is important to be able to think critically, always to recognise flaws in articles, arguments or work that I see.					
4. It is important that I understand myself and question why I am doing this research.					
5. I think I manage my own and others' emotions appropriately.					
6. I keep copies of records of each meeting with my supervisor.					
7. I want to continue working in this discipline when I have finished my studies.					
8. I want to demonstrate an independence of mind.					
9. I expect to become a different person, to be changed or transformed by the research work I am doing.					
10. I enjoy being with my research supervisor and other students.					
11. I like to send my supervisor something to read before I meet with them, to demonstrate I am making progress.					
12. It is important that I understand the work of key researchers in my field.					
13. It is important that I am able to put forward counter-arguments to propositions.					
14. I may go through periods of self doubt, a 'dark night of the soul' whilst doing my research, but I will emerge the stronger for it.					
15. It is important that I maintain positive working relationships with other departmental staff and help them as required.					
16. I note in my diary key dates for annual reports etc, so I can monitor my progress.					
17. I look for examples of interesting and excellent work in my field to emulate.					
18. I believe that successful researchers are able to think in a broad or interdisciplinary way.					
19. I think it is important to learn to reframe the important questions.					
20. I can enthuse others by my interest in my work.					

Table 8.16b Score sheet – add the scores up and it will give you some idea of your priorities as a doctoral student

Q no	Score	Q no	Score	Q no	Score	Q no	Score	Q no	Score
1		2		3		4		5	
6		7		8		9		10	
11		12		13		14		15	
16		17		18		19		20	
Total function score		Total enculturation score		Total critical thinking score		Total emancipation score		Total relationships score	

Chapter 9

Looking to the future

Researching and developing research supervision skills

There are many pressures on research in the curriculum. At an undergraduate level it is resource intensive, time hungry and difficult to assess in a consistent way. At the other end of the higher education scale, major pressures on the doctorate include concerns about its purpose and completion rates (sometimes called attrition). At all levels there are growing moves to harmonise education across Europe.

Concerns about how to maintain or develop standards are international, averting and detecting plagiarism is harder with the massification of education and, as was argued in Chapter 8, introducing research into the curriculum is one way of making plagiarism less possible. However there are broader questions about research ethics that need to be borne in mind. It is when supervising students doing research that we have the opportunity to explore what ethical research needs to consider.

Using the framework to explore ethics in research supervision

As we have seen in Chapters 2, 3 and 7, many ethical questions arise when supervising students doing research. It is only possible to use the framework to begin to explore these questions, but it can act as a useful prompt to help the academic check their 'ethical thermometer'. Students undertaking substantial research for the first time are entering an environment where it is entirely appropriate to highlight the difficult ethical dilemmas that researchers of the future might face. Difficult questions such as: do you carry on with an experiment that might create some substance that could be used for negative purposes, how do you manage a situation where research results might undermine a current commercial or national success story, what do you do if you suspect a colleague of falsifying their results?

Macfarlane (2009) has written a thoughtful book that explains clearly why it is so important to create our own independent ethical framework. He gives examples of the dreadful experiments carried out by various regimes under the guise of the greater national good. We follow duty ethical requests because we feel we have to, not because we feel they are right, and such behaviour can lead us to carry out unethical experiments.

Table 9.1 has an example of the type of prompts that this framework could encourage us to follow up with our students. There is also a helpful glossary of terms at the end of the chapter.

A challenge to the skills agenda

Another major influence has been the employability agenda. In the UK there have been several powerful Government initiatives to enhance transferable skills in higher education, they include: the Skills Agenda, the Roberts programme 'SET for success' (2002) and the Dearing Report (1997) leading to the introduction of Personal Development Planning (PDP).

In the UK, the introduction of the Joint Skills of the Research Councils and Arts and Humanities Research Board's Skills Training Requirements for Research Students (2002: 11) set out the following common view of the skills and experiences of a typical research student. The research student is expected to be able to manage research projects, validate problems, communicate to a range of audiences, maintain an open-minded, disciplined and thorough attitude, develop and maintain co-operative networks and teams and have a commitment to developing transferable skills and their own continuing professional development (Scott, Brown, Lunt & Thorne 2004: 17–18). This is a good place to begin, but if, as I maintain, at this level we are educating tomorrow's leaders, we have to ask whether it is enough.

The Roberts report emphasised the need for high-calibre PhD students and highlighted them as the academic or business researchers of tomorrow, and a key ingredient in our universities' future success.

In response to the Roberts Review, the Government announced substantial increases in the stipend for research council funded PhD students – from the 2003–04 minimum of £9,000 to a £12,000 minimum by 2005–06. The training of PhD students was also given close attention. The Roberts Review looked at the need for high standards of PhD work, adequate supervision of students, and training in transferable skills. The Review recognised that this might lead to some universities specialising in providing graduate schools and in time, this might play into a model where postgraduate degree-awarding powers are restricted to successful research consortia (Roberts Review 2002).

Universities were asked to develop progress files which were to be documents that enable all students to monitor, build and reflect upon their personal development (Dearing 1997).

The UK national Quality Assurance Agency (QAA) guidelines state that personal development planning (PDP) is concerned with learning in a holistic sense (both academic and non-academic) and they discuss a process of self-

Table 9.1 Some ethical considerations prompted by the framework

Functional	Enculturation	Critical thinking	Emancipation	Relationship development
What university codes of conduct should both the supervisor and student be aware of? Who owns the research data and any intellectual property that might arise from the research? What are the data storage regulations?	What professional body codes of conduct should both the supervisor and the student be aware of? What are the disciplinary expectations of replication? How might working in different cultures raise different ethical considerations?	What intellectual virtues are important – what does 'discovering the truth' mean in this context? How much relevance do the Aristotelian virtues such as episteme, nous, sophia and techne have?	What moral virtues are applicable: respectfulness, resoluteness, humility, sincerity and reflexivity (Macfarlane 2009)?	What boundaries need to be observed? What does the academic do if appropriate boundaries are passed? What does the academic do if they see colleagues making inappropriate decisions?
What duty or normative ethics apply?	What discourse do we share, how can we get it right?	How can we critique relevant deontological principles (like the Ten Commandments)?	How does this research fit with global ethics?	How does my relationship with students, research subjects and colleagues stand up to the scrutiny of virtue ethics?
Which ethics committees need to be consulted for this piece of research?			What sort of person should I be, and how will this research support that development?	

reflection, recording and planning to achieve personal objectives (QAA 2001). The guidelines also give statements about the intended purpose of PDP, i.e. to enable students to become more effective, independent and confident self-directed learners, to understand how they are learning, to relate their learning to a wider context and to improve their general skills for study and career management.

This approach to skills development for those studying higher degrees in research (HDR) has been challenged in Australia, where a study funded by ALTC has argued that a conventional competency-based approach is not appropriate for employability, and they have called for 'diversity, flexibility, quality and engagement' (Cumming & Kiley 2009).

We are also educating postgraduates to be leaders in a global and mobile world; the majority of them do not become researchers, some move into education as teachers or academics and 50 per cent move into other public services or business (Ball, Metcalf, Pearce & Shinton 2009). In these fast-moving times I have suggested that we need to be much more ambitious for our graduates and postgraduates.

The thesis of this book is that we need to focus on how we educate the globally competent graduate or postgraduate. Some of the skills they need to learn are familiar to us: the ability to design research projects; skills of analysis and academic writing; the ability to find, assimilate and synthesise large amounts of information on any given subject; the ability to manage a project ethically and present findings intelligibly. These are the given skills that we would expect every student to have. I suggest we need a broader base and a higher aspiration.

Our postgraduate students need to understand the philosophy of knowledge, as it is interpreted in their discipline and in others; they need to understand how that knowledge will be created and used in different societies, the sociology and politics of knowledge creation. Students who are engaged in cross-disciplinary research can have real problems if confronted by academics who are used to one way of thinking and one recommended approach to conducting the research. They need to be able to anticipate, analyse and make reasoned judgements about the disciplinary and ethical issues that are going to arise in the work that they seek to do.

Career management is one of the elements that does come through all three of the initiatives mentioned above, and our postgraduate students need to have some understanding of the different paths that they might follow, how many different careers they might undertake, how to identify, manage and protect all their assets and develop the personal skills and insights necessary to maximise their abilities. Arguably every postgraduate student needs a grounding in law so that they can understand contracts in different countries and how intellectual property is viewed.

It is our research-competent postgraduates that I think will form the pool of people from whom our future leaders will be drawn, so they need to develop a strategic vision, they need to anticipate at least some of the effects of their research and learn how to influence governments, businesses and the voluntary sector. For example, the leading engineer needs to confront the ethical question of how their work might be used, and if their research created environmental damage, they might feel obliged to move into the interdisciplinary area of life-cycle analysis and environmental research. They also need to be looking to their future and asking how they can build capacity to continue the important research that they have begun.

In some cases the aspirational list that follows favours the multilingual, high-flying generalist more than the bench researcher who just wants to work in a laboratory or at a computer. Whilst we need brilliant minds that can do brilliant research, we also need brilliant people to apply and develop that work – which is where the hitherto frequently undervalued professional doctorates might come in.

Is this the globally competent postgraduate?

Researcher skills

- Research design and methods
- Methods of analysis
- Academic writing
- Literature searches
- Project management
- Ethical issues
- Presenting findings (orally and in writing).

Philosophy of knowledge

- How knowledge emerges
- Sociology and politics of knowledge creation
- Philosophical approaches to ethical issues
- Disciplinary and interdisciplinary ways of thinking
- Enculturation in different cultures/disciplines.

Career management

- What is an academic?
- Career path options
- Understanding life phases
- Creating a cycle of credibility
- Asset management
- Financial planning, grant applications and fundraising
- Networking skills

- Intellectual property and patent law.

Strategic planning and communication

- Teaching and learning
- Influencing large numbers of people (via media and in organisations)
- Influencing government
- Large-scale project management (where there are many powerful stakeholders)
- Team-working and networking
- Political/social/strategic analysis skills
- Intercultural issues including language and education
- Research cultures and building research capacity
- The role of public service.

If this is a reasonable list to aim for, how do we enable this level of development, are any parts compulsory and how do we assess it? The purpose of creating the list is to help the academic enable the student to make knowledgeable choices about the more generic skills and knowledge they want to develop, and when. Another reaction to this list is that it is too demanding, that it requires a research student to acquire skills and knowledge that it has taken others a lifetime to acquire. Exactly so. Education is also about enabling students to learn what it has taken others a lifetime to acquire.

The researcher development framework

Vitae UK have developed a researcher development framework (RDF) which will be of interest to those who want to stay in academic life (www.vitae. ac.uk). It takes account of the Joint Skills Statement (http://webarchive. nationalarchives.gov.uk/+/http:/www.hm-treasury.gov.uk/set_for_success. htm) and the Concordat (the document agreed between employers and educators to support the career development of researchers (www. researchconcordat.ac.uk). Their RDF was created from empirical data collected through interviewing researchers to identify the characteristics of excellent researchers. It has four domains and each domain has up to five phases which could be said to indicate development from an early career researcher to a star researcher (or even a Nobel Prize winner). The four domains it examines are:

1 Knowledge and intellectual abilities: this looks at the subject knowledge, research methods and theoretical knowledge, practical application of research methods, information seeking, management, literacy and languages. It then explores cognitive abilities which include analysing, synthesising, critical thinking, evaluating and problems solving, and

explores creativity (which it defines as having an inquiring mind, intellectual insight, the capability to innovate, construct arguments and take intellectual risk).

2   Engagement, influence and impact: this looks at engagement from a local to an international scale, from collegiality and team-working, through people management, supervision, leadership, collaboration, equality and diversity, communication, publication, teaching, public engagement, enterprise, policy formation and global citizenship.

3   Research governance and organisation: this looks at many of the functional approaches to research such as health and safety, ethical practices, attribution and co-authorship, Intellectual Property Rights (IPR) and copyright, respect and confidentiality, attribution and co-authorship, project planning and management, risk management, income generation, financial management, managing infrastructure and resources.

4   Personal effectiveness: this explores many of the qualities that we have looked at under 'relationship development' – enthusiasm, perseverance, integrity, self-confidence, reflection and ability to take responsibility. It then explores issues around self-management including prioritisation, commitment to research, time management, responsiveness to change and ability to manage a work–life balance, followed by looking at the ability to manage one's own career through continuing professional development, responsiveness to opportunities, networking, building reputation and esteem. (See RDF at www.vitae.ac.uk)

There is also a downloadable CPD tool that enables researchers to chart their progress across the domains and highlight areas for further development. This is available at: http://vitae.ac.uk/researchers/1272-291211/RDF-CPD-tool.html Another use for the RDF is to enable researchers to articulate the skills they are developing, and if they are seeking employment outside research then that articulation could be helpful if those skills can be transformed into the language of and to meet the priorities of the potential employer.

Development opportunities for research supervisors

The most fundamental influence on a research supervisor is their own experience as a research student. The supervisors interviewed for this study gave evidence which supported the view that the primary influence on neophyte supervisors is how they themselves were supervised (Delamont *et al.* 2000, Brew & Peseta 2004).

However, that experience is not very useful unless it is conceptualised. A conceptual model helps the supervisor to deal with a variety of different situations, whereas an unreflective copying of how one was supervised (or deliberately avoiding the way one was supervised) may not.

> One of the things that really strikes me is that I quite often expect people to get stuck in places that I got stuck. I know that sounds a stupid thing to say as it is not logical, because people don't ... so I expected her to get stuck in the lit review because I found that so difficult, but she got stuck on the methodology ... (Soft applied)

The framework described in this book can provide a neutral language for academics to discuss together their priorities at any particular time during the process of supervising research. Some opportunities for academics to explore how their conceptions might affect their practice include:

1 *Action learning:* groups of experienced and/or inexperienced academics can meet regularly to discuss problems and share good practice. This approach was successfully used with experienced medical doctors, enabling them to reflect on how they were relating with patients and why some relationships were causing more problems than others (Balint 1957). The structure can be based on action learning principles where each member of staff has their own dedicated time and support from the group to explore their own issues. These groups can be departmentally based or cross-disciplinary and they work well with 6–8 people and an experienced facilitator. This latter suggestion may seem an unattainable luxury in your department but a termly lunch-time session – to which a member of the staff development team is invited, perhaps would be a good start.

2 *Workshops:* these are probably the most frequently used forms of training and development activities. Leeds Metropolitan University offer workshops for new universities covering admissions, supervising part-time and distance learning students, ethical issues and university procedures. Newcastle University reported running workshops for experienced and inexperienced supervisors which, one year, through force of circumstance, had to be combined. They were much more successful with a mix of experience and have been run this way ever since (Taylor & Beasley 2005: 29). An excellent set of case studies from John Wakeford is included in Eley and Murray (2009: 108–199).

3 *Scholarly seminars:* these are often enticing, but the lure of the 'quick fix of merely listening to advice' is rarely enduring. Mechanisms for examining the scholarly proposals at an institutional or departmental level need to be in place before the seminar happens.

4 *Researching and reflecting on good practice:* this can help to surface and disseminate ideas. Essentially this is the approach taken in a very structured way by Brew and Peseta (2004). They provided case studies

and then supported participants in writing and reflecting on their own experience. This can be done on-line, as a blended learning experience, or via face-to-face teaching.

5 *Developing/updating policy:* bringing together experienced supervisors (with recent students and/or newer supervisors) to review or update policy or strategy can provide a learning experience for all involved. A short series of occasional meetings could enhance the practice of everyone and could take into account new issues such as the impact of the Bologna process, and supervision by skype, web-cam or email.

6 *Writing case studies:* writing up a case study can be a useful reflective task on its own, but they can be further used in on-line programmes, or as exercises for pairs or small groups of supervisors to discuss.

7 *Mentoring programmes:* a mentoring programme for established supervisors to mentor new supervisors or contract researchers who are also supervising can be supportive both for the mentee and the mentor. A mentoring programme including a written mentoring agreement where roles are clearly allocated (using the framework) and time set aside for discussion about the supervision process can also be useful leadership training for the mentor. Some occasional meetings for the mentors to share their experiences can create an increased awareness of how they can best develop new supervisors.

8 *Accredited and assessed programmes:* in the UK the Staff and Educational Development Association (SEDA) and the Higher Education Academy (HEA) can accredit programmes. SEDA has accredited a ten-week programme delivered at the University of the Arts in London. The programme takes a functional approach and includes a series of afternoon sessions covering such topics as the values and purpose of research degrees, recruitment, managing, monitoring and documenting the process, assessment and supervisor career needs. It is assessed, each supervisor is expected to have a mentor and one of its key objectives is to create a network of support for supervisors. Pearson and Brew (2002) recommend a longer and much more comprehensive training programme which also looked in detail at the pedagogy of supervision and evaluation of the process. Some universities offer research supervision as a module of a postgraduate certificate for all academic staff. TAPPS (Training and Accreditation Programme for Postgraduate Supervisors) offers training for doctoral supervisors (originally established by the BBSRC, the Biotechnology and Biological Sciences Research Council) at the Institute for Animal Research in Surrey (Eley & Murray 2009: 173). In Sweden doctoral students are entitled to have a trained research supervisor and there are extensive assessed academic development programmes. In 2010, six higher education institutions (HEI) in Ireland have combined to pilot a training framework for supervisors of research postgraduate students, and this comprises a

series of four workshops spread over 17 contact hours. This programme covers both institutional specific practices, the PhD student life-cycle (including supporting academic writing) and advanced topics such as managing a large research group, external examining and intellectual property issues.

A variety of approaches to training supervisors are being used around the world. Brew and Peseta (2004) describe one of the few programmes which are formally assessed. At the University of Sydney they offered six 'supervision modules' each of which took an hour and a half of independent study time. This was then followed by the 'Recognition Module' which was an on-line reflective case study of the participants own supervision in practice, demonstrating their learning journey with on-line feedback as the writing was in progress. Through using the writing of case studies with feedback to inform and develop practice, they illustrated a movement towards a more student-centred view of supervision (Brew & Peseta 2004: 16).

Experienced academics, as well as novices, need the opportunity to meet other academics and supervisors from across the university to continue to discuss what does and what does not work. Departments vary enormously in their collegiality, some being best described as the 'Marie-Celeste' and others being hives of activity from dawn to dusk. Often the nature of the discipline dictates whether or not the department work is a solitary or group activity, but it is also a matter of management style and communal resources.

Leonard (2007) argued that the departmental culture has an influence. She said that an 'academically and socially inclusive culture which enables students to make contacts and develop networks, can have a positive impact on student motivation, experience and outcomes'. She points out that, while some departments do work specifically to develop collegiality among students, being a part-time student, having international status and poverty can all be excluding factors which require even greater effort on the part of the university. Developing collegiality amongst academics and nurturing our new supervisors is also important work for the department to undertake. Some senior academics set out the culture of their team quite clearly:

> I am looking for (academics) who are happy to work at the boundaries (of my discipline) that have got interesting ideas, who are committed to the kind of work we do in this unit, which is a bit unusual. There is quite a lot of commitment, to be involved in the seminar programme, come on the Monday, to do supervision every week for the first year, there is a lot of commitment ... and I am upfront about that. (Soft applied)

There are also financial awards offered for good supervisory practice. The University of Sydney is one of many Australian universities with awards for excellence. The criteria for receiving an award include interest and enthusiasm for supervising, integrating students into the research community, accessibility, clear goals, time management and a repertoire of skills (Taylor & Beasley 2005: 210).

Developing skills in supervision needs to be tackled in various ways and to form part of the ongoing continuing professional development (CPD) for academics. In what continues to be a turbulent environment there is a need for even experienced supervisors to update their skills and share their experiences. In 2003, the University of Edinburgh introduced a requirement that staff had to undertake at least one day of continuing professional development every five years in order to remain in good standing as a supervisor (Taylor & Beasley 2005). In most universities, this type of development is voluntary, if it is available at all.

The QAA Code of Practice (2004) says that new supervisors will participate in specified development activities and existing supervisors will demonstrate continuing professional development. Supervisors working in industry or professional practice should be included in developmental activities. These developmental activities can create an ideal opportunity for creating and developing an academic team.

Further developments: applying the framework to teaching and learning

The origins of this work come from the one-to-one supervision experience, and in this book I have extended it to cover supervision of students doing research at various levels in higher education. The original interviewees and the academics who have participated in workshops with me have demonstrated great enthusiasm for interrogating and extending the applications of the framework. This energy has led me to ask two questions: firstly are these five dimensions akin to powerful archetypes in teaching and learning (at least in western cultures) and secondly can we tap the enthusiasm for research and channel it into wider teaching and learning situations?

If the answer to either of these questions is 'yes' then it is justified to explore how these five approaches might disaggregate the skills required for teaching at a masters level. There is concern at the moment about the variable nature of the courses in teaching and learning in higher education that we encourage (and in some countries, insist) that our academics take. The research that Lee and Pettigrove (2010) undertook led to recommendations for a holistic approach. The question that emerges from Table 9.2 is: does this begin to identify a curriculum for the development of new academics?

Table 9.2 identifies mainly instrumental skills, the 'tools of the trade', and implicitly argues that academic staff need an understanding of all of these items before they begin teaching. However, as many have shown and reported (Biggs & Tang 2007, Prosser & Trigwell 1999, Ramsden 2003), it is our underlying conceptions of what teaching and learning are about that actually influence how we teach. We can also use the framework to tease out some of these underlying beliefs (see Table 9.3).

These underlying beliefs would lead to some very practical actions. If the functional approach was being followed to teaching and learning in HE, the academic might be making sure that they planned their lectures a year in advance and that every lecture linked to the preceding and succeeding ones. They would be negotiating with the library and administration to ensure that there is access to all key resources, especially books, journals, web-based activities, laboratory equipment and teaching rooms. They would be able to map every learning activity to a relevant learning outcome and would collect student feedback on a regular and comparable basis. They might also map their student's grades against a range of factors (for example: teaching plans, added value statistics and completion rates).

Where the enculturation approach was important the academic might be giving students a framework to help them complete their assignments, ensuring that experienced students are involved in passing on and monitoring the rules of the laboratory or other norms. They might be introducing their students to key authors and giving them biographical information about them. They may be particularly conscious of the needs of international students, and sometimes their families.

If critical thinking was the approach that was valued, we might see the academic saying that they regularly set up student debates, encourage students to work with other disciplines and to assess the similarities and differences between them. They may be encouraging students to create assessment criteria and to get involved in marking other students' work in order to develop their critical skills.

Where education is seen by the academic as an emancipatory act, they might be intentionally leaving it to students to take the initiative because it would be important that their students discover their own intrinsic motivation. If students wanted to work in a different way, they would usually encourage them and if a student fails the attitude would be 'how can we learn from this?' They would see themselves much more as a facilitator than a guide or leader.

The academic who is working from a relationship approach might be concerned to ensure that there are attractive places available for students to meet socially. They may go for coffee with their students and encourage beginning and end of term or semester social engagements. They would want to know if their students were facing difficulties outside the programme and would be happy to talk appropriately about how they managed their own studies and dealt with both success and failure.

Having reviewed some practical actions, we can go one layer deeper with this form of analysis to look at core beliefs about how people learn and the values that inform these core beliefs (Table 9.4). As throughout this book, I am not arguing that any of these are mutually exclusive, but I am suggesting

Table 9.2 Some requirements for teaching and enabling learning at higher education levels

Functional	Enculturation	Critical thinking	Emancipation	Relationship development
Curriculum and assessment design	Designing induction programmes for students	Subject knowledge and pedagogical knowledge of how learning happens in the discipline	Introducing research in the curriculum	Participating in and initiating social events
Lecturing and large-group teaching skills	Organising department seminars and conferences		Supporting enquiry-based learning	Reflection on appropriate self-disclosure and boundaries
Tutoring and small-group teaching skills	Finding and sharing examples of good practice in the discipline	Giving students the tools for self and peer assessment	Engaging with personal development planning	Skills in managing conflict
Giving feedback	Understanding how students learn in different cultures	Comparing the criteria for validity in own subject with others	Encouraging metacognition and reflection	
Quality assessment issues				
Institutional codes of practice, e.g. on diversity, plagiarism, health and safety		Attending/organising journal clubs		
Use of institutional equipment and web-based technology				

Table 9.3 Some underlying beliefs about teaching and learning in higher education

	Functional	Enculturation	Critical thinking	Emancipation	Relationship development
Role of the lecture	Logical giving of information	Introduction of key texts and people in the discipline	Explain how to evaluate, validate and challenge	Point to some sources of information, encourage exploration	Welcome Create learning partnerships
Underlying approaches to teaching	Prescriptive, possibly didactic	Inclusive, participatory, demonstrating good practice	Analytical, theoretical, conceptual	Enabling, empowering	Friendship Altruism Co-inquirer
Core beliefs about learning and knowledge	Learning is about the accumulation of knowledge	Learning is demonstrated by engaging in academic/ professional/ disciplinary practices	Learning is about developing cognitive skills	Learning is about discovery	Learning is about shared development

that if we make them transparent, and encourage academics to reflect on what values they hold most dear, we may enable them to expand their range and thus reach some students who may be operating from a different belief system.

Perhaps the most controversial element that arises from Table 9.4 is that it highlights the power of love in education. Earlier in this book I have given plenty of warnings about the boundaries that need to be observed, but I am also arguing that (when the other approaches are mastered) for many students 'relationship development' is the most powerful category of all. This is perhaps best encapsulated by the professor who said:

> Is there anyone who has not been transformed by encountering at least one teacher in their life who has made them feel special and that they are capable of great things? For some of us, that is all it takes: just that one teacher. (Hard applied)

Conclusion

Developing the academics who educate our research students is a noble cause because it is their students who form the engine of our future. This book leaves partially unanswered the question about how an academic who is (necessarily) steeped in their own world, can have a rich panoply of experiences which enable them to educate the leaders of the future (the discussion in these pages about the options of delegating of this role to others, arranging introductions where possible and exploring the potential of the programme, work experience and research project to create employability are only parts of the answer). We need more research on academic and other careers, so that our research students can discover their own occupational fertility.

The academic does have a profound influence on the student, but it is limited, and sometimes it helps to realise the extent of the other influences on the student. McAlpine and Norton (2006) have written about the nest of influences surrounding students; there is much that is not under our control or our responsibility and Figure 9.1 illustrates how many of these influences are overlapping.

Good academics and good supervisors surround themselves with good teams, everyone has a part to play and identifying and drawing on that is part of the skill. Then the academic takes one more step to developing an intellectual legacy, maybe creates an academic family and certainly consolidates their own identity.

In the process of doing this, the university is rewarded by having vibrant research teams, becoming a place that more good academics want to work in and more good students want to study at.

Table 9.4 Applying the framework to understanding core beliefs and values

	Functional	Enculturation	Critical thinking	Emancipation	Relationship development
Beliefs about how people learn	Structured goal-oriented process	Emulating, replicating	Theorising, analysing	Discovering Constructivism	Being affirmed
Values	Practical applicability	Belonging	Reasoning Rigour	Autonomy	Love Agape

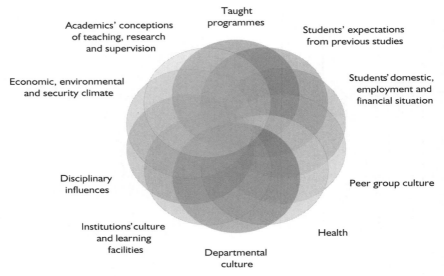

Figure 9.1 Some of the many influences on the student

Even though disciplines evolve, bureaucracy requires formulae and managers and governments change, we will always depend upon outstanding students becoming the people who discover what we need for the future. The message of this book is: master the functional, that is not difficult; then use all the other approaches in any combination that seems appropriate at the time, and enjoy the intoxicating feeling that comes from your own success and developing students who, if you do it well, will become even more successful than you can imagine. There are two key questions that I have been asked, to which (for once) there are simple answers.

Q1: What, in your experience, is the most important approach?
A: *It is the **flexibility** to adapt and combine that is most important.*
Q2: Are there any common characteristics of bad supervisors?
A: **Inflexibility.**

The framework that has been explored in this book has covered some very diverse literature and inevitably specialists in one element of it may find that section superficial. I have described only one way of conceptualising supervision and research with larger samples may identify outliers and other factors which challenge and deepen our understanding. In addition to this, comments from readers to help enhance any future editions will be welcome.

Recommended reading for research students

Cryer, P. (2006) (3rd Edition) *The Research Student's Guide to Success*. Maidenhead: McGraw Hill.

Macfarlane, B. (2009) *Researching with Integrity: The Ethics of Academic Enquiry*. New York. Routledge.

Murray, R. (2006) (2nd Edition) *How to Write a Thesis*. Maidenhead: Open University Press.

Murray, R. (2009) (2nd Edition) *How to Survive your Viva. Defending a Thesis in an Oral Examination*. Maidenhead: Open University Press.

Phillips, E. M., and Pugh, D. S. (2005) (4th Edition) *How to Get a PhD*. Buckingham: Open University Press.

Useful web sites

Dublin Descriptors (2004) describing the first, second and third cycles of Higher Education as part of the Bologna Process, available at: http://www.hochschulkurs. de/qm1_2005_schneider_dublin.pdf (accessed 5 December 2010).

National framework for qualifications (2008) is available at: http://www.qaa.ac.uk/ academicinfrastructure/FHEQ/EWNI08/default.asp (accessed 5 December 2010).

SEEC 2003 level descriptors are available at http://www.seec-office.org.uk/ SEEC%20FE-HECLDs-mar03def-1.doc (accessed 5 December 2010).

Kiley (2000) Expectations in supervision questionnaire available for download from the UK Vitae website and from: http://researchsuper.cedam.anu.edu.au/sites/ researchsuper.cedam.anu.edu.au/files/Expectation%20Rating.pdf (accessed 5 December 2010).

The Oxford Learning Institute has developed an excellent set of resources on research supervision, available at: http://www.learning.ox.ac.uk/rsv.php?page=289 (accessed 5 December 2010). This web site will be kept up to date with any future findings, resources and publications: www.drannelee.wordpress.com

Glossaries to help further inquiry

The terms in these glossaries (Box 9.1) are allocated to the five different approaches so that if the reader wants to study a particular approach further, there are signposts available. In practice, however, the application of these terms is not confined to just one approach.

Key terms mostly related to the functional approach

Advisor: academic advisors act as personal and/or academic tutors and as supervisors to postgraduate student's research projects in some countries. In the USA a research supervisor is called an advisor.

Credits: a credit measures both the quantity and quality of learning and in the UK equates to 120 hours. Level 7 is typical of the learning expected at masters and level 8 is typical of the learning expected at doctoral level.

Marking criteria: a set of criteria that are applied to assessed work. They can be defined in a series of subcategories, e.g. literature search; knowledge and content; compliance with instructions; synthesis, conceptualisation, conclusions communication and presentation, referencing.

Masters degree: a course of postgraduate study typically made up from 180 credits of which most have to be at level 7 and the rest can be at level 6 (see QAA.ac.uk). The masters programme can be a taught programme or achieved by research (M Phil).

Module: some universities offer courses made up from modules, or blocks of learning, measured by credits. A module will have learning at one particular level.

Module leader: the academic who is in charge of planning the teaching and assessment for the module, and who will oversee students' progress through that particular part of the course.

PhD (Doctor of Philosophy): a programme of research at doctoral level.

Postgraduate certificate: typically 60 credits at masters level.

Postgraduate diploma: typically 180 credits at masters level.

Programme accreditation: a programme can be made up from a series of modules and will have a number of credits. Each university will have an accreditation procedure to check that the programme will be taught at the required level and the students and staff will have the necessary resources.

Practitioner Doctorate: a programme of study at doctoral level which includes taught courses and research in an applied field. It includes the following qualifications: Doctor of Business Administration (DBA), Doctor of Clinical Practice (DClinPrac), Doctor of Education (EdD), Doctor of Engineering (EngD) and Doctor of Psychology (PsychD).

Professional doctorate: doctorates that focus on embedding research in a reflective manner into another professional practice. These are the same as practitioner doctorates.

Supervisor: the academic who is responsible for ensuring that the university fulfils its responsibilities to the student.

Key terms in ethical thinking

Codes of practice: These are produced by professional bodies to give guidelines for good practice and to create a rulebook for identifying unethical behaviour. They are related to duty ethics because they are ultimately imposed. They arise out of normative ethical approaches.

Deontological ethics: Deontological ethics argues that ethical meaning is found in principles such as the 'Ten Commandments' or the Kantian imperative to 'treat equals equally and unequals unequally' which can apply in all situations. An action is right or wrong, independent of the consequences and the end does not justify the means (Gregory 2006a).

Discourse ethics: Ethical meaning emerges from discourse enabling reflection on values and the discovery of shared norms. Getting the discourse right would therefore be of the highest priority (see Habermas 1992).

Duty ethics: Duty ethics are not a true ethical stance, a person who does their duty because they feel obliged to, that they ought to, is not necessarily acting morally.

Global ethics: Global ethics builds on the sense of connectedness stressed by the feminist ethics; it stresses responsibility for the environment and humankind globally.

Normative ethics: Normative ethics takes on the more practical task of arriving at moral standards that regulate right and wrong conduct. This may involve articulating the good habits that we should acquire, the duties that we should follow, or the consequences of our behaviour on others.

Teleological ethics: In contrast to deontological ethics, utilitarianism argues that the end does justify the means. Utilitarianism is a consequential theory. The utility (hedonic) calculus suggests calculations about the right decision can be made on the basis of intensity, duration, certainty, extent, remoteness, richness and purity.

Virtue ethics: Virtue ethics looks at a person's character. It asks, 'what sort of person should I be?' Commonly held values are the Rogerian attributes of 'integrity', 'respect for others' and 'empathy'. The Aristotelian attributes include truthfulness, modesty, temperance (balance and moderation), rightful indignation, courage and justice.

Key terms mostly related to enculturation

Apprenticeship: an opportunity to learn by practical experience, working with skilled and experienced people at their trade, art, or calling.

Coaching: instructing and directing intensively.

Communities of practice: a group of people with a common purpose – joining this group requires a process of socialisation.

Enculturation: the process of socialisation into the discipline, the working milieu (e.g. the academic department and the university) and the national culture. A person is 'enculturated' when they are comfortable being or working at all these levels; they have learned the traditional content of a culture and assimilated its practices and values. Their membership of the relevant groups is accepted and others may seek their advice on such matters. It usually requires a long period of study and an ability to acquire tacit knowledge.

Epistemology: the theory or philosophy of knowledge. In the context of this book it particularly applies to the epistemology of different disciplines and will include an understanding of boundaries, presuppositions and an agreement about what is to count as valid knowledge.

International student: any student who is studying in a culture that is not native to them, and who may be unused to the food, language and predominant religious or cultural practices.

Legitimate peripheral participation: the first stage of inviting a newcomer to become a member of a community. It is a low-risk invitation which usually has a social element to it (e.g. attending conferences); it is about learning to talk with other members of the community. There is an element of apprenticeship and socialisation, before being able to become a full participant in the community.

Ontology: a branch of metaphysics concerned with the nature of being, the study of the essence of things. In the context of this book it refers particularly to someone who instinctively reacts as a member of a disciplinary community. They have become a member of the discipline (as opposed to merely having an epistemological understanding of it).

Tacit knowledge: hidden knowledge which is not easily articulated but which is a powerful contributor to how people think and act. It is transmitted socially through being a member of a community. New members of any community need to be aware of tacit knowledge to be able to participate effectively. This is not propositional or scientific knowledge.

Key terms mostly related to critical thinking

Concept maps: a diagrammatic depiction of a set of concepts and the relationships between them.

Deductive reasoning: reasoning from a general statement or definition to a particular instance.

Dialectical thinking: elements considered in relation to each other. A court hearing or a debate are examples of dialectical thinking.

Dialogical thinking: a discussion (or dialogue) about an issue from different perspectives or frames of reference.

Epistemology: the philosophical study of theories of knowledge.

Inductive reasoning: reasoning from a particular instance or fact to a general conclusion.

Knowledge: the act of having a clear perception or understanding. It is based on understanding and skill, which are, in turn, based on thought, study and experience. Knowledge cannot be divorced from thinking minds. It is produced, analysed, evaluated, maintained and transformed by thought. A book contains knowledge only in the derivative sense – it only exists because minds can access it. Knowledge is not to be confused with recall.

Metacognition: awareness of the thought processes being used.

Proposition: a larger unit of analysis than a concept, defined as a statement that expresses relationships among concepts and that has a truth value.

Socratic questioning: a deeply probing technique intended to uncover meaning, truth, understanding or beliefs.

Syllogism: a deductive inference consisting of two (or more) premises which are assumed to be true, and a conclusion. A syllogism can create a misleading impression as in the following example: Cows eat grass; grass is eaten by cows; so all grass is eaten by cows.

Key terms mostly related to emancipation

Authenticity: coming out or being open about one's feelings. When the academic owns his or her feelings, they are said to be 'congruent'.

Emancipation: to be freed or liberated from oppression.

Empathy: sensing the student's private world (e.g. fear, confusion, elation) as if it were your own.

Mentor: a trusted, key person to help reflection. The mentor can help by encouraging questioning of the governing variable(s), support the mentee in their journey from the known into uncharted territory, and focus on learning opportunities.

Mentoring: an emancipatory act. Although the term 'mentor' has been appropriated in some professions to include notions of assessment, the pure conception of mentoring is to encourage personal growth.

Personal development planning: a conscious process of identifying and recording personal and professional development needs and planning to meet them.

Self efficacy: the influence of beliefs on behaviour influenced by verbal encouragement, role and self modelling.

Transformative learning: the process of changing beliefs, attitudes and values in response to the acquisition of knowledge. Sometimes seen as the main goal of adult learning.

Unconditional positive regard: an unevaluative, warm acceptance and liking of the student as a person.

Key terms mostly related to relationship development

Altruism: a benevolent concern for others, selflessness. Whether or not genuine altruism exists has been hotly contested, some argue that ulterior motives of self-interest hide behind altruism.

Boundaries: a border or perimeter of a psychological entity. Sometimes crossed without awareness. The phrase 'boundary management' is used by psychoanalysts.

Emotional intelligence: the ability to use emotions for human connection. This is another contested term which frequently includes concepts of self-awareness, an ability to read others' feelings and emotional resilience.

Friend: a person whose company one finds pleasurable, who reinforces self-esteem.

Trust: a confident attitude towards another person which can arise from experience and which can imply knowledge, affection, respect and/or reverence. Personal disclosure can build interpersonal trust.

References

Abernethy, A. (2006) 'Rethinking the PhD in English' in Golde, C. M., and Walker, G. E. (eds) *Envisioning the Future of Doctoral Education: Preparing Stewards of the Discipline*. San Francisco, CA: Jossey-Bass.

Åkerlind, G. (2008) 'A phenomenographic approach to developing academics' understanding of the nature of teaching and learning'. *Teaching in Higher Education*. 13.6: 633–644.

Argyris, C. and Schon, D. A. (1974) *Theory in Practice: Increasing Professional Effectiveness*. San Francisco, CA: Jossey-Bass.

Balint, M. (1957) *The Doctor, the Patient and His Illness*. London: Pitman Medical.

Ball, C., Metcalf, J., Pearce, E., and Shinton, S. (2009) *What do PhDs do?* Cambridge: CRAC.

Bandiera, O., Larcinese, V., and Rasul, I. (2010) 'Heterogenous class size effects: new evidence from a panel of university students'. *The Economic Journal* 120.December: 1365–1398 http://www.res.org.uk/economic/freearticles/2010/december2010.pdf (accessed 03 January 2011).

Bandura, A. (1994) 'Self-efficacy'. *Encyclopaedia of Human Behaviour*. 4: 71–81. http://www.des.emory.edu/mfp/BanEncy.html (accessed 29 November 2009).

Barnett, R. (1997) *Higher Education: A Critical Business*. Buckingham: SRHE/Open University Press.

Barnett, R. (2000) *Realizing the University in an Age of Supercomplexity*. Buckingham: SRHE/Open University Press.

Barnett, R. (2004) 'Learning for an unknown future'. *Higher Education Research and Development*. 23.3: 247–260.

Barnett, R. (2009) 'Knowing and becoming in the higher education curriculum'. *Studies in Higher Education*. 34.4: 429–440.

Barrie, S. C. (2004) 'A research-based approach to generic graduate attributes policy', *Higher Education Research and Development*. 23.3: 261–275 http://www.itl.usyd.edu.au/graduateattributes (accessed 11 March 2011).

Barrie, S. C. (2006) 'Understanding what we mean by the generic attributes of graduates'. *Higher Education: The International Journal of Higher Education and Educational Planning*. 51.2: 215–241, http://www.itl.usyd.edu.au/graduateattributes (accessed 11 March 2011).

Baxter Magolda, M. B. (1992) *Knowing and Reasoning in College: Gender-Related Patterns in Students' Intellectual Development*. San Francisco, CA: Jossey-Bass.

Beaty, L. (2003) *Action Learning*. York: Generic Centre.

Becher, T. and Trowler, P. (1989) (2001 edition cited) *Academic Tribes and Territories*. Buckingham: SHRE/Open University Press.

Belenky, M. B., Clinchy, B. M., Goldberger, N. R., and Tarule, J. M. (1986) *Women's Ways of Knowing: The Development of Self, Voice and Mind*. New York: Basic Books.

Berglass. S. (2002) 'The very real dangers of executive coaching'. *Harvard Business Review* June 80.6: 86–93.

Biggs, J. and Moore, P. (1993) *The Process of Learning*. Sydney: Prentice Hall.

Biggs, J. and Tang, C. (2007) *Teaching for Quality Learning at University*. 3rd edition. Buckingham: SRHE/Open University Press.

Biglan, A. (1973a) 'The characteristics of subject matter in different scientific areas'. *Journal of Applied Psychology*. 57.3: 195–203.

Biglan, A. (1973b) 'The relationships between subject matter characteristics and the structure and output of university departments'. *Journal of Applied Psychology*. 57.3: 204–213.

Bologna Declaration (1999) Bologna Declaration on the European space for higher education: an explanation: http://ec.europa.eu/education/policies/educ/bologna/bologna.pdf (accessed 29 November 2009).

Boud, D., Keogh, R., and Walker, D. (1985) 'Promoting reflection in learning: a model', in Boud, D., Keogh, R., and Walker, D. (eds) *Reflection: Turning Experience Into Learning*. London: Kogan Page.

Bourdieu, P. (1986) 'The forms of capital', in Richardson, J. G. (ed.) *Handbook of Theory and Research for the Sociology of Education*. New York : Greenwood Press.

Bourdieu, P. (1998) *Practical Reason*. Oxford: Polity Press.

Boyer, E. (1990) *Scholarship Reconsidered: Priorities of the Professoriate*. San Francisco, CA: Jossey-Bass.

BPS (2006) *Code of Ethics and Conduct*. Leicester: British Psychological Society.

BPS (2008) *Professional Practice Guidelines*. Leicester: British Psychological Society.

Breau, S. (2009) personal communication.

Brennan, J. and Shah, T. (2003) *Report on the Implementation of Progress Files*. London: Centre for Higher Education Research and Information.

Brew, A. (2001) 'Conceptions of research: a phenomenographic study'. *Studies in Higher Education*. 26.3: 271–285.

Brew, A. (2006) *Research and Teaching: Beyond the Divide*. Basingstoke: Palgrave Macmillan.

Brew, A. and Peseta, T. (2004) 'Changing postgraduate supervision practice: a programme to encourage learning through reflection and feedback'. *Innovations in Education and Teaching International*. 41.1: 5–22.

Brookfield, S. (1995) *Becoming a Critically Reflective Teacher*. San Francisco, CA: Jossey-Bass.

Browne, M. N. and Freeman, K. (2000) 'Distinguishing features of critical thinking classrooms'. *Teaching in Higher Education*. 5.3: 301–309.

Burden, P. and Lee, A. (2006) *Personal Development Planning: A Resources Guide for Academic Staff*. Guildford: University of Surrey.

Burke, R. (2005) *Project Management Planning and Control Techniques*. 4th edition. Chichester: John Wiley and Sons.

Calderhead, J. and Gates, P. (1993) *Conceptualising Reflection in Teacher Development*. London: Falmer Press.

Carr, W. and Kemmis, S. (1986) *Becoming Critical: Education, Knowledge & Action Research*. Lewes: Falmer Press.

Carroll, J. (2002) *A Handbook for Deterring Plagiarism in Higher Education*. Oxford. Oxford Centre for Staff and Learning Development.

Carson, B. H. (1996) 'Thirty years of stories: The professor's place in student memories'. *Change*. 28.6: 10–17.

Chartered Institute of Personnel Development (CIPD) (n.d.) Psychological Contracts http://www.cipd.co.uk/subjects/empreltns/psycntrct/psycontr.htm?IsSrchRes=1 (accessed 29 November 2009).

Clarkson, P. (1995) *Change in Organisations*. London: Whurr Publishers.

Clutterbuck, D., and Ragins, B. R. (2002) *Mentoring and Diversity*. Oxford: Butterworth Heineman.

Code of Practice for Research Degrees (2000) Guildford: University of Surrey.

Cousin, G. (2009) *Researching Learning in Higher Education*. New York and Abingdon: Routledge.

Cousin, G. and Deepwell, F. (2005) 'Designs for network learning: a communities of practice perspective'. *Studies in Higher Education*. 30.1: 57–66.

Cowan, J. (2008) *On Becoming an Innovative University Teacher: Reflection in Action*. Buckingham: SHRE/Open University Press.

Cox, M. D. (2008) 'Faculty and professional learning communities placed in Wenger's community of practice model'. London, 7th International Conference on Scholarship of Teaching and Learning (15 May 2008).

Cumming, J. (2010) 'Doctoral enterprise: a holistic conception of evolving practices and arrangements'. *Studies in Higher Education*. 35.1: 25–39.

Cumming, J. and Kiley, M. (2009) *Research Graduate Skills Project*. Strawberry Hills, NSW: Australian Learning and Teaching Council. http://www.altc.edu.au/resource-research-skill-development-questions-anu-2009 (accessed 05 December 2010).

Daniels, H. (2008) *Vygotsky and Research*. Abingdon: Routledge.

Darling, L. A. (1985) 'What do nurses want in a mentor?'. *Journal of Nursing Administration*. 14.10: 42–44.

Dearing, R. (1997) *Higher Education in the Learning Society*. Norwich: HMSO.

Delamont, S., Atkinson, P., and Parry, O. (2000) *The Doctoral Experience: Success and Failure in Graduate School*. London: Falmer Press.

Denicolo P., Fuller M., and Berry D, (2010) *A Review of Graduate Schools in the UK*. Lichfield: UKCGE

Dewey, J. (1933) *How We Think: A Restatement of the Relation of Reflective Thinking to the Educative Process*. Lexington, MA: D.C. Heath.

Donald, J. G. (2002) *Learning to Think*. San Francisco, CA: Jossey-Bass.

Drake, P. and Heath, L. (2011) *Practitioner Research at Doctoral Level*. London: Routledge.

Egan, G. (2002) *The Skilled Helper*. Pacific Grove, CA: Brooks/Cole Thomson Learning.

Eley, A. and Jennings, R. (2005) *Effective Postgraduate Supervision*. Maidenhead: Open University McGraw-Hill Education.

Eley, A. and Murray, R. (2009) *How to Be an Effective Supervisor*. Maidenhead: Open University McGraw-Hill Education.

Elkana, Y. (2006) 'Unmasking uncertainties and embracing contradictions', in Golde, C. M., and Walker, G. E. (eds) *Envisioning the Future of Doctoral Education: Preparing Stewards of the Discipline*. San Francisco, CA: Jossey-Bass.

Elton, L. and Pope, M. (1989) 'Research supervision: the value of collegiality'. *Cambridge Journal of Education*. 19.3: 267–276.

EMC (2008) Code of Ethics. European Mentoring Council. http://www.emccouncil.org/fileadmin/documents/EMCC_Code_of_Ethics.pdf (accessed 29 November 2009).

Engstrom, Y. (1996) 'Developmental work research as educational research'. *Nordisk Pedagogik: Journal of Nordic Educational Research*. 15.5: 131–143.

Engstrom, Y (2001) 'Expansive learning at work: toward an activity theoretical reconceptualisation'. *Journal of Education and Work*. 14.1: 133–156.

Entwistle, N. (2007) *Research into Student Learning and University Teaching*. British Journal of Educational Psychology Monograph. Series II.4: 1–18. Leicester: British Psychological Society.

Eraut, M. (2007) *Early Career Earning at Work and its Implications for Universities*. British Journal of Educational Psychology Monograph Series II.4: 113–133. Leicester: British Psychological Society.

EUA (2005) *Doctoral Programmes for the European Knowledge Society*. Brussels: European Universities Association.

EUA (2007) *Doctoral Programmes in Europe's Universities: Achievements and Challenges*. Brussels: European University Association.

Firth, A. and Martens, E. (2008) 'Transforming supervisors? A critique of post-liberal approaches to research supervision'. *Teaching in Higher Education*. 13.3: 279–289.

Freeman, R. (1998) *Mentoring in General Practice*. Oxford: Butterworth Heinemann.

Freire, P. (1970) *Pedagogy of the Oppressed*. (Trans. Myra Bergman) New York: Seabury Press.

Gatfield, T. J. (2005) 'An investigation into PhD supervisory management styles: Development of a dynamic conceptual model and its managerial implications'. *Journal of Higher Education Policy and Management*. 27.3: 311–325.

Gibbs, G. (2010) *Dimensions of Quality*. York. Higher Education Authority. Available at http://www.heacademy.ac.uk/assets/York/documents/ourwork/evidence_informed _practice/Dimensions_of_Quality.pdf (accessed 4 December 2010).

Golde, C. M. (2007) 'Signature pedagogies in doctoral education: are they adaptable for the preparation of education researchers?'. *Educational Researcher*. 36.6: 344–351.

Golde, C. M. and Walker, G. E. (eds) (2006) *Envisioning the Future of Doctoral Education: Preparing Stewards of the Discipline*. San Francisco, CA: Jossey-Bass.

Grant, B. M. (2005) The Pedagogy of Graduate Supervision: Figuring the Relations between Supervisor and Student. PhD Thesis. Aotearoa: University of Auckland.

Grant, B. M. (2008) 'Agonistic struggle: master–slave dialogues in humanities supervision'. *Arts and Humanities in Higher Education*. 7.1: 9–27.

Gregory, J. (2006a) Ethics and Professional Practice in Coaching. Unpublished paper for MSc in Change Agents Skills and Strategies. Guildford: University of Surrey.

Gregory, J. (2006b) 'Facilitation and facilitator style,' in Jarvis, P. (ed.) *The Theory and Practice of Teaching*. 2nd edition. Routledge: London.

Grenyer, B. F. S. (2002) *Mastering Relationship Conflicts: Discoveries in Theory, Research, and Practice*. Washington, DC: American Psychological Association.

Guest, D. E., and Conway, N. (2002) 'Communicating the psychological contract: an employer perspective'. *Human Resource Management Journal*. 12.2: 22–38.

Habermas, J. (1992) *Postmetaphysical Thinking*. Cambridge: Polity.

Halse, C. and Malfroy. J (2010) 'Retheorising doctoral supervision as professional work'. *Studies in Higher Education*. 35.1 79–92.

Hargreaves, J. (2008) 'Risk: the ethics of a creative curriculum'. *Innovations in Education and Teaching International*. 45.3: 227–234.

Harkin, J. (1998) 'Constructs used by vocational students in England to evaluate their teachers'. *Journal of Vocational Education and Training: The Vocational Aspect of Education*. 50.3: 339–353.

Harrison, R. (2002) *Learning and Development.* 3rd edition. London: Chartered Institute of Personnel Development.

Hattie, J. and Marsh, H. W. (1996) 'The relationship between research and teaching: a meta-analysis'. *Review of Educational Research.* 66: 507–542.

Hawkins, P. (2006) 'Coaching supervision' in Passmore, J. (ed.) *Excellence in Coaching.* London: Kogan Page.

Healey, M. and Jenkins, A. (2009) *Developing Undergraduate Research and Inquiry.* York: Higher Education Academy.

HEPI (2004) *Postgraduate Education in the United Kingdom.* Oxford: Higher Education Policy Institute.

Herman, L. and Mandell, A. (2004) *From Teaching to Mentoring: Principle and Practice: Dialogue and Life in Adult Education.* London: Routledge Falmer.

Heron, J. (1999) *The Complete Facilitator's Handbook.* London: Kogan Page.

Heron, J. (2001) *Helping the Client.* London: Sage.

Hockey, J. (1994) 'New territory: problems of adjusting to the first year of a social science PhD'. *Studies in Higher Education.* 19. 2: 177–190.

Hockey, J. (1996) 'Contractual solution to problems in the supervision of PhD degrees in the UK'. *Studies in Higher Education.* 21.3: 359–371.

Holbrook, A., Bourke, S., Fairbairn, H., and Lovat, T. (2007) 'Examiner comment on the literature review in PhD theses'. *Studies in Higher Education.* 32.3: 337–356.

Hutchings, W. (2007) *Enquiry-based Learning: Definitions and Rationale.* Centre for Excellence in Enquiry-Based Learning Essays and Studies, University of Manchester. Available from http://www.campus.manchester.ac.uk/ceebl/resources/papers/hutchings2007_definingebl.pdf (accessed 29 November 2009).

Hyman S. E. (2006) 'The challenges of multidiscipinarity: neuroscience and the doctorate', in Golde, C. M., and Walker, G. E., (eds) *Envisioning the Future of Doctoral Education: Preparing Stewards of the Discipline.* San Francisco, CA: Jossey-Bass.

Ives, G. and Rowley, G. (2005) 'Supervisor selection or allocation and continuity of supervision: PhD students' progress and outcomes'. *Studies in Higher Education.* 30.5: 535–555.

Jackson, C. and Tinkler, P. (2007) *A Guide for Internal & External Doctoral Examiners.* London: Society for Research into Higher Education.

Jackson, T. E. (2001) 'The art and craft of "gentle Socratic" inquiry,' in Costa, A. (ed.) *Developing Minds: A Resource Book for Teaching Thinking.* Alexandria, VA: Association for Supervision and Curriculum Development.

Jarvis, P. (2006) *Towards a Comprehensive Theory of Human Learning.* London and New York: Routledge.

Jenkins, A., Healey, M., and Zetter, R. (2007) *Linking Teaching and Research in Disciplines and Departments.* York: Higher Education Academy.

Johnson, D. W. and Johnson, R. T. (2001) 'Co-operation and conflict: Effects on cognition and metacognition,' in Costa, A. (ed.) *Developing Minds: A Resource Book for Teaching Thinking.* Alexandria, VA: Association for Supervision and Curriculum Development.

Jones, A. (2009) 'Redisciplining generic attributes: the disciplinary context in focus'. *Studies in Higher Education.* 34.1: 85–100.

JQI (2004) Shared 'Dublin descriptors' for Short Cycle, First Cycle, Second Cycle and Third Cycle Awards. Joint Quality Initiative Report. European Universities Association. http://www.eua.be/fileadmin/user_upload/files/EUA1_documents/dublin_descriptors.pdf (accessed 29 November 2009).

Kamler, B. and Thomson, P. (2006) *Helping Doctoral Students Write.* London: Routledge.

Kember, D. (2000) 'Misconceptions about the learning approaches, motivation, and study practices of Asian students'. *Higher Education.* 40.1: 99–121.

Khan, P. and O'Rourke, K. (2004) *Guide to Curriculum Design: Enquiry-based Learning.* York: Higher Education Academy.

Kiley, M. (2006) 'Expectation' particularly in a cross-cultural postgraduate research experience. Unpublished paper for supervisor workshops. Canberra: Australia National University.

Kiley, M. (2009) 'Identifying threshold concepts and proposing strategies to support doctoral candidates'. *Innovations in Education and Teaching International.* 46.2: 293–304.

Kinchin, I. M., and Hay, D. B. (2007) 'The myth of the research-led teacher'. *Teachers and Teaching: Theory and Practice.* 13.1: 43–61.

King, P. M., and Kitchener, K. S. (1994) *Developing Reflective Judgement: Understanding and Promoting Intellectual Growth and Critical Thinking in Adolescents and Adults.* San Francisco, CA: Jossey-Bass.

Kleiman, P. (2008) 'Towards transformation: conceptions of creativity in higher education'. *Innovations in Education and Teaching International.* 45.3: 209–217.

Koch Christensen, K. (2005) Bologna Seminar. Doctoral programmes for the European Knowledge Society. Salzburg, 3–5 February. General Rapporteur's Report. http://www.eua.be/eua/jsp/en/upload/Salzburg_Report_final.1129817011146.pdf (accessed 29 November 2009).

Kram, K. E. (1985) *Mentoring at Work: Developmental Relationships in Organisational Life.* Glenview, IL: Scott, Foresman and Company.

Krause, E. (2007) '"Maybe the communication between us was not enough": Inside a dysfunctional advisor/L2 advisee relationship'. *English for Academic Purposes.* 6: 55–70.

Kulej, G. and Park, C. (2008) PRES 2008 Initial Results. Higher Education Academy Annual Conference, Harrogate (01 July 2008).

Lave, J. and Wenger, E. (1991) *Situated Learning: Legitimate Peripheral Participation.* Cambridge: Cambridge University Press.

Leach, J. and Moon. B (2008) *The Power of Pedagogy.* Los Angeles, CA: Sage.

Lee, A. (2006) 'Can you recognise a good facilitator when you see one?'. *Educational Developments.* 7.3 July. London: SEDA http://epubs.surrey.ac.uk/info_sci/2/ (accessed 29 November 2009).

Lee, A. (2007) 'How can a mentor support experiential learning?'. *Journal of Clinical Child Psychology and Psychiatry.* 12.3: 333–340. http://epubs.surrey.ac.uk/info_sci/4/ (accessed 29 November 2009).

Lee, A. (2008a) 'How are doctoral students supervised? Concepts of research supervision'. *Studies in Higher Education.* 33.4: 267–281.

Lee, A. (2008b) *Supervision Teams: Making Them Work.* London: Society for Research into Higher Education.

Lee, A. and Green, B. (2009) 'Supervision as metaphor'. *Studies in Higher Education.* 34.6: 615–630.

Lee, A. and Pettigrove, M. (2010) *A Review of Provision for Graduate Teaching Assistants.* Lichfield: UK Council for Graduate Education.

Leonard, D. (2001) *A Woman's Guide to Doctoral Studies.* Buckingham: Open University Press.

Leonard, D. (2007) 'The doctoral student experience: the influence of departmental context'. Unpublished paper given to the Oxford Learning Institute on 06 July 2007 (see also Leonard, D. and Becker, R. (2009) 'Enhancing the doctoral experience at the local level' in Boud, D. and Lee, A. (eds) *Changing Practices of Doctoral Education*. Abingdon: Routledge).

Levy, P. (2009) Inquiry-based learning: a conceptual framework (version 4). Sheffield: Centre for Inquiry-based Learning in the Arts and Social Sciences, University of Sheffield. Available from: http://www.shef.ac.uk/cilass/ (accessed 29 November 2009).

Lovitts, B. (2008) 'The transition to independent research: who makes it, who doesn't and why'. *The Journal of Higher Education*. 79.3: 296–325.

Macfarlane, B. (2009) *Researching with Integrity: The Ethics of Academic Enquiry*. New York: Routledge.

Manathunga, C. and Goozee, J. (2007) 'Challenging the dual assumption of the "always/already" autonomous student and effective supervisor'. *Teaching in Higher Education*. 12:3: 209–222.

McAlpine, L. and Norton, J. (2006) 'Reframing our approach to doctoral programs: an integrative framework for action and research'. *Higher Education Research and Development*. 25.1: 3–17.

McAlpine, L., Jazvac-Martek, M., and Hopwood, N. (2007) Doctoral Student experience: Events that contribute to feeling like an academic/belonging to an academic community. Paper presented to the Society for Research in Higher Education Annual Conference, December 2007.

Meyer, J. and Land, R. (eds) (2006) *Overcoming Barriers to Student Understanding: Threshold Concepts and Troublesome Knowledge*. Abingdon: Routledge.

Mezirow, J. (1991) *Transformative Dimensions of Adult Learning*. San Francisco, CA: Jossey-Bass.

Moon, J. (2000) *Reflection in Learning and Professional Development: Theory and Practice*. London: Kogan Page.

Moon, J. (2004) *A Handbook of Reflective and Experiential Learning: Theory and Practice*. London: Routledge Falmer.

Morgan, G. (1997) *Images of Organizations*. 2nd edition. London: Sage.

Mortimore, P. (ed.) (1999) *Pedagogy and its Impact on Learning*. London. Sage.

Morton-Cooper, A. and Palmer, A. (2000) *Mentoring, Preceptorship and Clinical Supervision*. Oxford: Blackwell Science.

Moseley, D., Baumfield, V. M., Higgins, S. E., Lin, M., Miller, J., Newton, D., Robson, S., Elliott, J., and Gregson, M. (2004) *Thinking Skills Frameworks for Post-16 Learners: An Evaluation*. London: LSDA.

Murphy, N., Bain, J., and Conrad, L. (2007) 'Orientations to higher degree supervision'. *Higher Education*. 53: 209–234.

Murray, M. and Owen, M. Q. (1991) *Beyond the Myths and Magic of Mentoring: How to Facilitate an Effective Mentoring Programme*. San Francisco, CA: Jossey-Bass.

Murray, R. (2006) *How to Write a Thesis*. Buckingham: Open University Press.

Murray, R. (ed.) (2008) *The Scholarship of Teaching and Learning in Higher Education (Helping Students to Learn)*. Maidenhead: Open University Press/McGraw-Hill.

Murray, R. (2009) *How to Survive Your Viva: Defending a Thesis in an Oral Examination*. 2nd edition. Maidenhead: Open University.

Neumann, R. (2003) *The Doctoral Education Experience: Diversity and Complexity*. Canberra: Department of Education Science and Training, Evaluations and Investigations Program.

Neumann, R. (2007) 'Policy and practice in doctoral education'. *Studies in Higher Education*. 43.4: 459–474.

OECD (2009) *Education at a Glance*. Paris: OECD Publications. http://www.oecd.org/dataoecd/41/25/43636332.pdf (accessed 29 November 2009).

Okorocha, E. (2007) *Supervising International Students*. London: Society for Research into Higher Education.

Palfreyman, D. (2008) *The Oxford Tutorial*. Oxford Centre for Higher Education Policy Studies. Margate: Thanet Press. Also available as OxCHEPS Occasional Paper No 1 at http://oxcheps.new.ok.ac.uk/Publications/theoxfordtutorial.html.

Pang, M. F. and Marton, F. (2005) 'Learning theory as teaching resource: enhancing students' understanding of economic concepts'. *Instructional Science*. 33.2: 159–191.

Park, C. (2007) *Redefining the doctorate – a discussion paper*. York: Higher Education Academy.

Pearson, M. and Brew, A. (2002) 'Research training and supervision development'. *Studies in Higher Education*. 27.2: 135–150.

Pearson, M. and Kayrooz, C. (2004) 'Enabling critical reflection on research supervisory practice'. *International Journal for Academic Development*. 9.1: 99–116.

Perkins, D. (1999) 'The many faces of constructivism'. *Educational Leadership*. 57.3: 6–11.

Perry, W. J. (1970) *Forms of Intellectual and Ethical Development in the College Years*. New York: Holt, Rinehart and Winston.

Phillips, E. M. and Pugh, D. S. (2005) *How to get a PhD*. 4th edition. Buckingham: Open University Press.

Popper, K. R. (1963) *Conjecture and Refutations: The Growth of Scientific Knowledge*. New York: Routledge.

Prosser, M. and Trigwell, K. (1999) *Understanding Learning and Teaching: The Experience in Higher Education*. Buckingham: Open University Press/Society for Research into Higher Education.

QAA (2001) *QAA Guidelines on HE Progress Files*. http://www.qaa.ac.uk/academicinfrastructure/progressFiles/guidelines/progfile2001.pdf (accessed 29 November 2009).

QAA (2004) *Code of Practice for the Assurance of Academic Quality and Standards in Higher Education. Section 1: Postgraduate Research Programmes*. http://www.qaa.ac.uk/academicinfrastructure/codeOfPractice/section1/postgrad2004.pdf (accessed 29 November 2009).

QAA (2008) QAA benchmark statements. http://www.qaa.ac.uk/academicinfrastructure/FHEQ/EWNI08/default.asp (accessed 29 November 2009).

Ramsden, P. (2003) *Learning to Teach in Higher Education*. 2nd edition. London: Routledge Falmer.

Rana, R. (2000) *Counselling Students: A Psychodynamic Perspective*. Basingstoke: Macmillan.

Ravenscroft, A., Wegerif, R., and Hartley, R. (2007) *Reclaiming Thinking: Dialectic, Dialogic and Learning in the Digital Age*. Learning through Digital Technologies. BJEP Monograph. Leicester: The British Psychological Society. http://www.interloc.org/pubs/RecthinkBJEPfinal.pdf (accessed 29 November 2009).

Research Councils and Arts and Humanities Research Board (2002) *Skills Training Requirements for Research Students*. London: RC and AHRB.

Roberts Review (2002) *Set for Success: The Supply of People with Science, Engineering and Technology Skills*. London: UK Government Department of Trade and Industry and Department of Education and Skills. http://www.vitae.ac.uk/policy-practice/1685/Roberts-recommendations.html (accessed 29 November 2009).

Rodriguez, L. and Cano, F. (2007) 'The learning approaches and epistemological beliefs of university students: A cross-sectional and longitudinal study'. *Studies in Higher Education*. 32.5: 647–667.

Rogers, C. (1967) *On Becoming a Person: A Therapist's View of Psychotherapy.* London: Constable.

Rogers, C. (1983) *Freedom to Learn in the 80s.* Columbus, OH: Charles E. Merrill.

Rousseau, D. M. (1995) *Psychological Contracts in Organisations: Understanding Written and Unwritten Agreements.* Thousand Oaks, CA: Sage.

Rowland, S. (2000) *The Enquiring University Teacher.* Buckingham: Society for Research into Higher Education and Open University Press.

Ryan, Y. and Zuber-Skerritt, O. (1999) *Supervising Postgraduates from Non-English Speaking Backgrounds.* Buckingham: SHRE/Open University Press.

Salovey, P. and Mayer, J. (1997) 'What is emotional intelligence?' in Salovey, P. and Sluyter, D. (eds) *Emotional Development and Emotional Intelligence: Implications for Educators.* New York: Basic Books.

Savin-Baden, M. (2008) *Learning Spaces.* Maidenhead: SRHE/Open University Press/ McGraw-Hill.

Schein, E. H. (1980) *Organisational psychology.* 3rd edition. Englewood Cliffs, NJ: Prentice Hall.

Schon, D. (1991) *The Reflective Practitioner.* Aldershot: Ashgate.

Schutz, W. (1984) *The Truth Option.* Berkeley, CA: Ten Speed Press.

Schutz, W. (2004) *The Human Element: Productivity, Self-esteem and the Bottom Line.* San Francisco, CA: Jossey-Bass.

Scott, D., Brown, A., Lunt, I., and Thorne, L. (2004) *Professional Doctorates: Integrating Professional and Academic Knowledge.* Maidenhead: Open University Press/McGraw-Hill/SRHE.

SEDA (2003) *Professional Development, Fellowship, Underpinning Values.* http://www.seda.ac.uk/index.htm (accessed 29 November 2009).

Senge, P. M. (1990) *The Fifth Discipline: The Art and Practice of the Learning Organization.* London: Random House.

Simpson, R. (2009) *The Development of the PhD Degree in Britain, 1917–1959 and Since.* New York: Mellen.

Smith, B. (1997) *Lecturing to Large Groups.* Birmingham: Staff & Educational Development Association.

Smith, D. (1999) 'Supervising NESB students from Confucian educational cultures,' in Ryan, S. and T. Zuber-Skerritt (eds) *Supervising Postgraduates from non-English Speaking Backgrounds.* Open University Press: Buckingham.

Spencer Oatey, H. and Stadler, S. (2009) *The Global People Competency Framework – Competencies for Effective Intercultural Interaction.* Coventry: University of Warwick, Centre for Applied Linguistics. Available from http://www.globalpeople.org.uk/ (accessed 29 November 2009).

Sternberg, R. J. and Lubart, T. (1995) *Defying the Crowd: Cultivating Creativity in a Culture of Conformity.* New York: Free Press.

Stevenson, P. and Brand, A. (2006) 'Exploring the developmental impacts of completing a postgraduate certificate in learning and teaching'. *Educational Developments.* 7.3: 18–19. London: SEDA.

Swartz, R. and Perkins, D. N. (1990) *Teaching Thinking: Issues and Approaches.* Pacific Grove, CA: Midwest Publications.

Taylor, E. W. (2007) 'An update of transformative learning theory: a critical review of the empirical research (1999–2005)'. *International Journal of Lifelong Education.* 26.2: 173–191.

Taylor, M. (1979) *Coverdale on Management.* London: Heinemann.

Taylor, S. (2009) 'The post-Humboldtian doctorate: implications for supervisory practice' in V. King, F. Deepwell, L. Clouder and C. Broughan (eds) *Academic Futures: Inquiries into Higher Education and Pedagogy.* Cambridge: Cambridge Scholars Publishing.

Taylor, S. and Beasley, N. (2005) *A Handbook for Doctoral Supervisors.* Abingdon: Routledge.

THES (Times Higher Education Supplement) (2009) *World University Rankings* 09 October. London: Times Higher Education.

Thomson, J. A. K. (2004) *Nicomachean Ethics* (revised by H. Tredennick). London: Penguin.

Thow, M. K. and Murray, R. (2001) 'Facilitating student writing during project supervision'. *Physiotherapy.* 87.3: 134–139.

Tinkler, P. and Jackson, C. (2004) *The Doctoral Examination Process: A Handbook for Students, Examiners and Supervisors.* Maidenhead: Society for Research into Higher Education and Open University Press.

Tosey, P. (2008) *Enquiry-based Learning: A Resource for Higher Education.* An ESCalate Publication for the Higher Education Academy. Bristol: ESCalate. http://escalate. ac.uk/downloads/4746.pdf (accessed 29 November 2009).

Tosey, P. and McDonnell, J. (2006) 'Mapping enquiry-based learning: Discourse, fractals and a bowl of cherries.' L2L Working Paper. http://www.som.surrey.ac.uk/ learningtolearn/documents/mappingEBL.pdf (accessed 29 November 2009).

Trafford, V. and Leshem, S. (2008) *Stepping Stones to Achieving your Doctorate: By Focussing on your Viva from the Start.* Maidenhead: McGraw-Hill/Open University Press.

Trowler, P. and Wareham, T. (2008) 'Tribes, territories, research and teaching: enhancing the "teaching–research nexus". Literature review'. York: Higher Education Academy. http://www.heacademy.ac.uk/assets/York/Trowler_Final_Report.pdf (accessed 29 November 2009).

Turner, P. and Curran, A. (2006) 'Correlates between bioscience students' experiences of higher education and the neurobiology of learning'. *Bioscience Education.* 7.5. http:// www.bioscience.heacademy.ac.uk/journal/vol7/Beej-7–5.pdf (accessed 21 December 2010).

Vardy, P. and Grosch, P. (1999) *The Puzzle of Ethics.* London: Fount.

Vilkinas, T. (2002) 'The PhD process: the supervisor as manager'. *Education & Training.* 44.3: 129–137.

Walker, M. and Thomson, P. (2010) *The Routledge Doctoral Supervisor's Companion.* London: Routledge.

Watson, D. (2009) *The Question of Morale: Searching for Happiness in University Life.* Buckingham: Open University Press.

Watts, J. H. (2010) 'Team supervision of the doctorate: managing roles, relationships and contradictions'. *Teaching in Higher Education.* 15:3: 335–339.

Weinstein, K. (1999) *Action Learning – A Practical Guide.* Aldershot: Gower.

Wisker, G. (2005) *The Good Supervisor.* Macmillan: Basingstoke.

Wisker, G. and Robinson, G. (2009) 'Encouraging postgraduate students of literature and art to cross conceptual thresholds'. *Innovations in Education and Teaching International.* 46.3: 317–330.

Index